Much Drinking in the Marsh

Also by Keith Swallow

The Book of Syn:
Russell Thorndike, Dr Syn and the Romney Marsh

Despite being born and raised in Surrey, Keith Swallow has had a lifelong obsession with both the coast and Romney Marsh. An auditor by profession, to relieve the crushing boredom of his working life he writes about Romney Marsh, runs marathons, is involved in local football administration and makes the occasional foray into public houses. He also follows the fortunes of Portsmouth Football Club and a number of other lost-cause sports teams. Now living near Rye in East Sussex, he has more opportunities to visit the Marsh and also indulge his hobby of sea kayaking. He is married with two grown-up children.

Much Drinking in the Marsh

A History of the Pubs and Breweries
of Romney Marsh

Keith Swallow

Edgerton Publishing Services
Pett, East Sussex

First published in Great Britain in 2017 by
Edgerton Publishing Services
Jasmine Cottage, Elm Lane, Pett, Hastings, East Sussex TN35 4JD
Tel. +44 (0) 1424 813003
Email enquiries@eps-edge.demon.co.uk

ISBN: 978-0-9933203-1-6

A CIP catalogue record for this book is available from the British Library.

Typeset in Garamond by Edgerton Publishing Services.

Printed and bound in Great Britain by Ashford Colour Press, Fareham, Hampshire?

Cover photographs
Front: Star, St Mary-in-the-Marsh
Rear:(top) Britannia, Dungeness (1980); signs left to right (top row): Three Mariners, Hythe; Bailiff's Sargeant, St Mary's Bay; New Inn. New Romney, Dymchurch; Shepherd & Crook, Dymchurch; Britannia, Dungeness; (bottom row): Plough, New Romney; Red Lion, Snargate; Pilot, Lydd-on-sea; Warren, New Romney; Duke's Head, Hythe

Contents

Author's Preface

It is not good practice to deal in clichés, but it really is the case that writing this book has, for me, been a labour of love. I not only have a deep and lifelong affection for Romney Marsh but also, for many years, have been a member of CAMRA (the Campaign for Real Ale). Whilst arguably symptomatic of an underlying alcohol dependency, this is also a reflection of my long-standing interest in pub history and culture. I have visited many Marsh pubs over the years and, whilst many are sadly no more, there are still some real gems to be found. My research has provided some fascinating insights into life on the Marsh, particularly in the post-war period. One of my favourite stories is recounted by Ken Oiller (part of the well-known Dungeness fishing family) in his book *Tales of an Ordinary Dungeness Man*. At the time (the late 1950s), he was taking a break from fishing and took a job as a bus conductor for Carey's, on the route between New Romney and Lydd, via Dungeness. It became the custom to drop off customers at pubs in Littlestone, Greatstone and Dungeness during the day and, on the final run, he would have to recall who had been dropped off where. A few blasts of the bus horn would signify drinking up time but, where some dedicated drinkers were concerned, Ken would have to go in and persuade them that they really had had enough! In the same part of the Marsh, another scene that will never again be witnessed is the spectacle of horse and dray deliveries to basic wooden pubs on Dungeness beach; the drays utilised encased cartwheels for ease of movement over the shingle (see the picture in Chapter 2). It is difficult to imagine such scenarios in today's faster-paced, automated and more impersonal times.

There are a few caveats that I would like to invoke. First, I have tried to capture any documented institution (alehouse, beerhouse, inn, tavern, pub or hotel) that has served alcohol to members of the general public. This includes some hotels, but restaurants and hotels that have served residents only – or have not offered a separate bar area – are excluded. Some early alehouses and beerhouses are not always easy to identify because they were generally not known by any special name, and directories that do exist prior to 1850 tend to list only the names of the owners.[1] Accordingly, unless other sources or histories exist, such places may have been overlooked. Further, some pubs have been demolished and rebuilt on adjacent sites, which causes extra confusion. There may also be omissions arising from source documents not identifying periods during which licences have been amended.

---

1. The definitive early source is *Bagshaw's 1847 Kent guide*.

Next, dates often need to be treated with extreme caution. Particularly where older pubs are concerned, there are sometimes conflicting accounts, and documentation may be either lacking or inconclusive. Even where provenance is not disputed, claims to be the oldest pub in a community still have to be treated with care as, in some cases, it is only a wall or other small part of the structure that remains of the original. Similarly, some pubs may be old but have not always continuously served the public in the same capacity. And some quoted closure dates overlook the reality that pubs often make a brave but short-lived and unsuccessful attempt to re-open.

For a combination of the above reasons, I have been reluctant to try and definitively quantify the number of pubs that have served the Marsh towns and villages. There is, too, the issue of just what comprises Romney Marsh. This is actually a generic term, encompassing the neighbouring Walland and Denge Marshes in addition to Romney Marsh proper (which lies to the north of a line drawn between New Romney and Appledore) and the East Guldeford Levels. In simpler terms, it is the shape of a slice of cake, following the course of the Royal Military Canal and bounded by Hythe at the northern end and Rye to the south.[2] But even this can give rise to debate: for example, Appledore is a village which sits right on the north-

Cheers! A timeless scene of locals unwinding at the end of the day (the Woolpack, Brookland)
Picture: courtesy Kent Messenger

2. Some dispute whether Rye is part of the Marsh, as it occupies higher ground, although the term "Rye and Romney Marsh" is frequently used. A few commentators extend the area past Rye to Pett Level, at the western end of the Canal. Whilst this also has some legitimacy for reasons of geology, they are in the minority.

ern bank of the Canal but which also has a station which is a mile inside this definition of the Marsh. In such cases I have tried to take a pragmatic approach.

Because I believe that pubs are an essential part of the community, I have grouped them by the communities that they serve, with an overview of the location to set the context. The chapters reflect categories which I hope make logical sense. Thus there are chapters dedicated to Rye; Hythe; Lydd and New Romney (the other two significant Marsh towns); coastal settlements; inland villages; and the Marsh environs.[3] Appendix 2 contains a list of all identified pubs, together with their current status.

Acknowledgements and Disclaimer

At the outset, I was confident that I knew most of the pubs in the area together with at least an outline of their histories but was soon proved – badly – wrong. A lot of contradictions also arise during research of this nature, and it takes proper local knowledge to sort the wheat from the chaff. In this, I am indebted to noted Romney Marsh historian Ted Carpenter for his input. Thanks are also due to Jill Walker, who has put me right on the fascinating background of the Rising Sun at Lydd; to Bill Coleman, whose family once owned the Star at Playden; to Rachel Joy for help with research; and to Colin and Margaret Walker of the Dymchurch Heritage Society, which does such an excellent job in terms of keeping local history alive – it is such a shame that not all villages have such dedicated individuals whose passion and dedication provide such an invaluable service for future generations.

Historic photographs have been assembled from numerous sources. Some have previously appeared several times in a number of different books, with few clues to their origin or copyright status. Whilst I assume that many may be out of copyright, a common denominator often appears to be Ted Carpenter. Many have come from his own vast collection or through sources connected to him; and I again thank Ted for his permission to use them. Where photographs have been taken from other single sources, I have endeavoured to track down the publisher, and I am similarly grateful to the *Kent Messenger* for their permission to use a number of images from their 1955 publication *Kent Inns: a Distillation*, and to *Kent Life* for their permission to use a photograph of the interior of the Butt of Sherry. Six more photographs have been taken from *Whitbread: the Inn Behind the Signs* by David Harper, whom I have tried unsuccessfully to contact. Paul Szabo-Davie, former owner of the Green Owl at Camber, has graciously allowed me access to his archives of local material; and further photographs have been taken from sites on the Internet that allow their sharing via a creative commons licence.

---

3. I have included any pub/hostelry that is within two miles of the generally accepted Marsh boundaries. It is a purely arbitrary definition.

Still others are previously unpublished and have been provided by individuals: I have credited these where appropriate. In a few cases, I have established that companies that previously held copyright have gone out of business, with no indication as to whether rights were transferred to others. If I have misrepresented ownership, I apologise unreservedly; the publisher will be pleased to make suitable arrangements to clear permissions with copyright holders it has not been possible to contact.

A book of this sort takes a long time to research. I cannot pretend that all the work has been arduous, although regret that I will no longer be able to say that I am popping out to "undertake research" rather than "going for a pint". But I should like to thank my family – Sue, Mark and Cathy – for their patience and forbearance. Finally, thanks to publisher David Penfold for his help and support.

Keith Swallow
January 2017

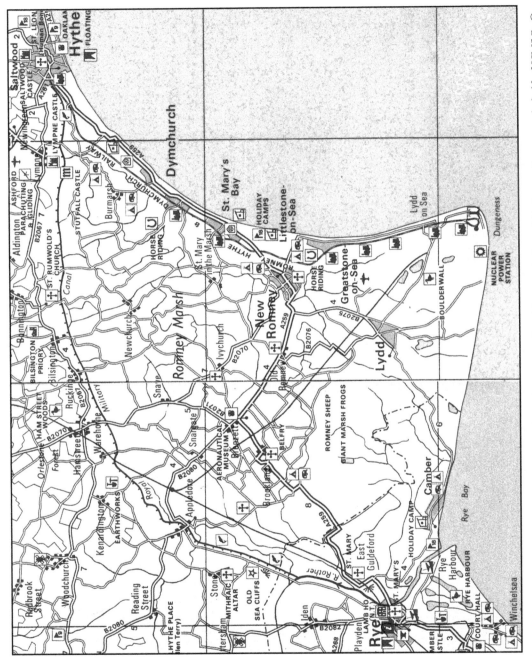

1

Overview of Marsh Breweries and Pubs

Breweries

It almost goes without saying that the pub could not exist without the brewery, which has in turn shaped its development. The history of brewing in England is well told by many sources, and that on Romney Marsh pretty much reflects the national picture. Early alehouses almost exclusively brewed on the premises but, by the 18th century, local independent breweries were the norm and most settlements of any size had their own. Such arrangements meant that breweries could respond to local tastes, and they also contributed to both local employment and economies. This changed with the advent of the railways and, with the passing of time, most communities additionally supported pubs supplied by larger regional brewers, which, typically, underwent significant consolidation throughout the 19th and (particularly) 20th centuries.

Within Kent, there have been a number of brewing strongholds. Maidstone and Faversham were the main centres, but Canterbury, Dover and the smaller town of Wateringbury have all been well represented at various times. Many of the local concerns have inevitably gone to the wall over the years: names that have themselves now become extinct but which would have been familiar to our forefathers include Style & Winch (Maidstone); Ash & Co. (Canterbury); Alfred Leney & Co (Dover); Frederick Leney & Sons (Wateringbury); Jude Hanbury & Co. Kent Brewery (also Wateringbury); and the East Kent Brewery Co. Ltd (Sandwich). All these supplied Marsh pubs, mostly during the 19th and early 20th centuries.

Hythe and Lydd Breweries

Of greater significance to this account were those breweries actually established on the Marsh. Little is recorded of the early history of James Pashley's Hythe brewery, apart from the fact that it began in 1699. But in around 1750 it appears that the business was acquired by John Friend of Ashford. Under his stewardship it prospered and by the mid-1770s Friend was supplying ale to about ten alehouses. By the turn of the 19th century, however, Friend was in poor health and too old to continue with the business. In 1801 (the year before his death) he sold the Hythe brewery and nine of the houses to William and Henry Mackeson of Deal. This was a momentous transaction in the history of brewing on Romney Marsh. The Mackeson brothers paid a substantial sum (£1200 for the "jewel in the crown" – The White Hart at Hythe – alone), but in so doing they shrewdly eliminated much of the former competition. The timing of this acquisition was either fortuitous or well judged, as the influx of British soldiers to counter the threat of French invasion resulted in a huge increase in demand for beer. Just a year later, the brothers expanded the enterprise by buying some land by the West Bridge to extend their premises. The Mackeson empire continued to expand throughout the century, and by 1820 owned some 20 pubs. Expansion continued and in 1875 – to meet even greater demand – the company additionally took on the lease of the nearby Sandgate Brewery.[1] In 1886, Mackeson's purchased the Tontine Brewery in Folkestone, as well as a further 16 public houses.

Hythe's Mackeson brewery, pictured around the turn of the 20th century

The Mackeson Brewery's best known product was Milk Stout, so named because of the sugar (lactose) within it. This was first brewed at Hythe in 1907 and, such was its popularity, a licence was granted to other brewers to produce it. It was advertised that each pint "contains the energising carbohydrates of ten ounces of pure dairy milk". More disturbingly, Mackeson's also claimed that its anti-rheumatic properties were "recommended by the medical profession"!

---

1.   The Sandgate Brewery had been established in 1836 and was on (naturally enough) Brewers Hill, close to the Clarendon Inn on a site now occupied by cottages.

The early advertising for Mackeson's Milk Stout displayed its Hythe origins

At its height, Mackeson's serviced some 140 tied houses within East Kent. Whilst the company clearly benefitted from its Hythe base being within easy reach of a number of hop fields, the same claim could not be made for Lydd; so it is quite a surprise that the latter also came to be a major brewing "player". The key to the appeal of Lydd to brewers, however, was a plentiful supply of very pure spring water, mainly in the area bounded by Vinelands and Elm Lodge. Commercial brewing in the town began in the High Street, possibly as early as the start of the 17th century.[2] By the 19th century these premises had been acquired by master brewer Alfred White, who ran the operation with his brother, Thomas.[3] And in 1832, in nearby New Street, Thomas Heisel set up a rival business at the back of the Rising Sun pub, which was soon after taken over by David Green and his wife, Catherine.[4] But the marriage had no surviving offspring and, after their deaths, David's sisters had no interest in taking on the business. Accordingly, at the end of 1861, the sisters sold out to Edwin Finn, a leading Lydd dignitary. This was an important landmark in Finn's life, launching a new and ultimately distinguished career.

Not many photographs of the old Finn's brewery exist, but this aerial shot of Lydd (left) clearly shows the brewery buildings at the bottom right. A working scene is depicted on the right

---

2. Whilst records are not conclusive, this would make it even older than the Hythe concern.
3. The Whites could fairly be described as entrepreneurs, as they also ran grocery and drapers' shops in the town.
4. *Bagshaw's Directory* shows Catherine Green as brewer and coal merchant residing here in 1847.

Meanwhile, back in Lydd High Street, Alfred White struggled on manfully alone after the death of his brother in 1849. By the time of Alfred's own death in 1878, Edwin Finn had already outgrown the limited facilities behind the Rising Sun and thus took the opportunity to acquire both the High Street Brewery and six pubs formerly owned by White. He also enrolled other family members into the undertaking. Finn completely redeveloped the site, and further built the business; a formal dinner held in June 1892 celebrated the opening of a brand new brewery. Finn's beers became renowned on the Marsh and, until quite recently, Finn's Pale Ale was still fondly remembered by older residents as "real beer." Finn – as the Mackeson brothers – was also to become a pioneer in experimenting with the carbonic acid gas given off from the vats and further made full use of the springs that came with the land to produce soft drinks and soda water. The latter was marketed under the name "Finn's Lydd Aerated Waters".[5]

At the height of their success, Edwin Finn & Sons owned 18 pubs on the Marsh alone, and their empire had spread far beyond. But, sadly, neither Mackeson's nor Finn's has survived. Mackeson's was bought out by Jude Hanbury in the 1920s, in a deal engineered by Whitbread (who later absorbed Hanbury), but brewing continued on the Hythe site until 1968. Mackeson's Milk Stout lives on in name, although its production has long since moved from its Kent roots and is currently brewed at Hydes in Manchester. For Finn's, the bubble also burst early in the 20th century. Competition had intensified and, by this time, Edwin Finn himself was in failing health. Even before his death in 1917, the writing was on the wall, and in 1921 the family sold the brewery together with 40 public houses and five off-licences by auction in London. The buyer was Style and Winch,[6] but former glories never returned to the Lydd site. Style & Winch in turn sold the business on to Kennards in 1935, who were unable to halt the decline, and brewing at Lydd stopped for good in 1937.

Other brewers and breweries

Another Marsh brewing centre was Rye. Although none of its enterprises rivalled either Mackeson's or Finn's in size, there were some significant concerns. The most prominent of these was the Eagle Brewery at Landgate, where, in addition to some of the old brewery buildings still surviving, the name lives on in the name of the street on which they stand. The Chapman brothers were also heavily involved, owning a number of pubs in the town and at one time operating from a site just across the parish boundary in East Guldeford. Meryon & Holloway and the Albion Brewery were also sizeable brewers in the town in the 19th century.

---

5. In addition, Finn's produced a celebrated ginger beer – although this was initially from the Rising Sun brewery site.
6. Style & Winch, by way of a number of acquisitions, eventually became part of the Courage brand.

Of other brewers synonymous with pubs in this part of the country, Fremlins stands out. Established in 1861 by the Fremlin brothers, it expanded significantly by taking over the entire estate of Frederic Leney & Sons in 1926/7.[7] Operating out of Maidstone and Faversham, the larger company, with its familiar elephant logo, established quite a foothold in the county, and a number of its former pubs still display some of the brewery's memorabilia – most notably the aluminium map sign depicting the self-styled region of "Fremlinshire". Although the Fremlins name was still in use for some time after, the company itself was absorbed by Whitbread in 1968.

East Guldeford Brewery in the late 19th century (left) and all that now remains – a wall incorporated within the Rye Lawn Tennis Club complex

Today, it is the name of "Britain's largest independent brewer", Shepherd Neame, that has come to dominate. "Shep's" is based at Faversham in north Kent and for a long time – as many an independent – it served only its close environs. But it grew significantly with the acquisition of a number of pubs in the mid-1970s, and further expanded when the 1989 Beer Orders[8] required the largest companies to reduce their tied pub stock. This resulted in Shep's investing heavily in pubs in the rest of Kent and over the border in Sussex, and its distinctive black and white signs can now be seen hanging over many a Marsh hostelry. There has also been something of a backlash against increasing globalisation and – partly aided by legislation – numerous micro-brewers have emerged in the last 30 years or so. Whilst these scarcely challenge the dominance of the large conglomerates, the requirement to allow guest beers has

7. Some sources show this as a merger, but, whatever the legal terminology, it was effectively a takeover.
8. This UK legislation restricted the number of tied pubs that large brewery companies could own, whilst also requiring large brewer landlords to allow a guest ale to be stocked (from outside the "tie"). One of the consequences was that smaller breweries were given the opportunity to expand, by picking off the pubs that its larger rivals were forced to shed. Although the Beer Orders were revoked in 2003, by this time the industry had been transformed. Prior to this time, Shepherd Neame had an interest in only four pubs on the Romney Marsh.

again changed the market to a degree. As a result, the Hop Fuzz Brewery at West Hythe (established by two young friends in 2011) is currently flourishing – and serving pubs throughout Kent and Sussex and even further afield. The beers of two other micros, both just off the Marsh – Rother Valley Brewing at Northiam and the Old Dairy (formerly at Rolvenden, but moving to larger premises in Tenterden in 2014) – also now regularly appear on the guest list of many a Marsh pub.

In April 2015 a further micro opened on a New Romney industrial estate, trading as the Romney Marsh Brewery. Initial signs are that this may in time play a bigger role on the Marsh brewing scene.

Marsh pubs

Context and history

Although there is often a view that the availability of pubs, taverns, inns and hotels in an area or town is a product of supply and demand, this is simplistic: the number of licensed premises in a community has been regulated to various extents over time. As early as the seventh century, Ethelbert, King of Kent, placed restrictions on the number of ale-sellers. The first real legislation came in in the tenth century, when King Edgar proclaimed that there should be no more than one alehouse[9] in a village, and introduced standard measurement. But by the 15th century there was again a proliferation of alehouses which – with justification – frequently began to be perceived as the territory of vagrants, thieves, harlots and prostitutes, and an Act of 1495 gave justices the power to deal and suppress. A further Act of 1552 gave authority to magistrates to license premises.

By the 17th century, the scene had changed again. The growth of transport resulted in the development of coaching inns in the smaller towns along the main routes leading out of London. This was partly responsible for fuelling a movement for the alehouses to offer better and more sophisticated facilities. As a result the term "public house" was introduced and from around 1750, "alehouse" tends to disappear from common usage. The public houses soon adopted the tavern and inn custom of dedicated drinking rooms with their own bar.

The 19th century saw a huge growth in licensed premises when – perversely – the government took action to try and control the supply of alcohol by effectively encouraging the ready availability of beer, through the 1830 Beerhouse Act. The reason for this apparent anomaly was the popularity of gin, which had been introduced by the Dutch. Whilst a heavy duty was imposed upon all imported gin, production in this country was unlicensed – and therefore cheap. It was the price of gin that led to it becoming the drink of choice for the working classes and to rampant alcoholism, and which resulted in calls for the government of the day

---

9. See Appendix I for definitions of alehouse and other drinking establishments.

to take action. Whilst Gin Acts of 1736 and 1751 had significantly reduced the consumption of gin, these had only short term success. Gin shops were prevalent, despite the attempts of brewers to open more alehouses

Particularly vociferous in opposition to the availability of alcohol were social reformers and the Church. A further driving factor was that, in an era that was undeniably sexist, gin was most favoured by women. Ale, however, was the favoured drink of the male (and often middle class) population, and therefore more "acceptable". Further, at this time ale was also in many quarters seen as harmless, nutritious and even healthy; and because local water supplies were often unsafe even children were encouraged to drink "small beer", a weaker version of the "adult" ale. Accordingly, the Beerhouse Act (or Beer Act) was designed essentially to counter the evils of gin, and was responsible for coining the term "beerhouse". The Act, in addition to lowering duty on beer, allowed any householder who paid rates to apply for a licence to sell beer or cider (spirits and wines were specifically excluded), normally from his front parlour. This licence was obtained direct from the Excise, bypassing the local magistrates who had – in many cases – previously abused their powers. It is strange, to say the least, that the authorities couldn't foresee the consequences of this action, one of which was rampant alcoholism. In the first year following the Act, 400 beerhouses opened across the country; and after eight years a staggering 46,000 had appeared, far outnumbering the combined total of the land's taverns, pubs, inns and hotels. Beerhouses often avoided traditional pub names and were called after the owner of the premises, or else adopted rather exotic names. But, before long, many of them had become little more than cheap lodging houses. This inevitably brought its own social problems, with drunkenness, violence and prostitution rife. A police report of one such beerhouse in Rye (where the number of licensed premises quadrupled between 1800 and 1870) collectively referred to its clientele as the dregs of society, but included a particular scourge: those desperados "who go mushrooming on the Romney Marsh"!

A number of beerhouses subsequently sought and were awarded full licences, but the authorities decided that this growth in licensed premises needed to be checked. The 1872 Licensing Act introduced restrictions on opening hours but, although proving very unpopular, did not directly result in many closures. However, the rise of the temperance movement and a further act of 1904 that gave police powers to recommend closure of "redundant" pubs did lead to a decline, although as seen in later chapters the police often abused this power. The end of the Great War in 1918 saw returning troops finding it difficult to secure and hold down peace-time employment; and, as often in times of hardship, people turned to drink in large numbers, with the demand for beer increasing dramatically. Yet, by 1932, a local newspaper reported that sales had dropped back to pre-war levels:

. . . mainly because of the economic climate and the excise duty which has raised beer prices to 7d a pint....output is now 52% below the level of 1910, and influential parties are taking the opportunity once more to persuade the Government to introduce prohibition. In Kent, hundreds of pubs have closed and breweries, feeling the pinch, are amalgamating.

Today, heavy levels of duty, allied with an economic downturn and reluctance by governments to halt the sale of cheap supermarket drink, have put different pressures on many pubs. The smoking ban that came into force in July 2007 has been put forward as another reason for their decline, although there is less evidence to support this argument, which has mainly been championed by the tobacco lobby. Whatever the legitimacy of this viewpoint, it cannot be denied that there is currently an alarming level of pub closures, with research commissioned by the Campaign for Real Ale (CAMRA) showing that – nationally – 31 a week were going to the wall in 2014.

CAMRA's concern is shared by many others, for the reason that pubs and inns have always played a major role in our society. Traditionally, the inn was the most important meeting place in any community: society meetings would be held here; weddings take place; and coroners' inquests and property auctions hosted. Inns also acted as a kind of early post office, holding parcels for collection, and later became important staging posts for the Royal Mail. The pubs and inns of Romney Marsh can collectively claim to have served all of these functions. And whilst they are not unique in this, because of both the remote communities that they have traditionally served and (in many cases) their proximity to the coast, they have over the years arguably assumed an even greater significance in the life of the ordinary person than is the case in many other parts of the country.

Smuggling

A factor that makes many Romney Marsh pubs stand out is their coastal location. For many of the communities, inns were also of course focal points for a thriving smuggling trade and served as hideouts for both smugglers and their contraband. Hardly any pub on the Marsh of sufficient vintage does not claim a link to the free trade, although those made for the Woolpack at Brookland, the Ship (Dymchurch), the Bell (Hythe), the Rose & Crown (New Romney) and the Mermaid (Rye) – to name but five – are *bona fide* and impressive. Of further interest is that some of the pubs that were once coastal are now a mile or more inland, as a result of land reclamation. Pubs such as the Woolpack, the Bell and the Warren at New Romney have fascinating histories (if no cellars!) and have had to adapt to changing circumstances.

Club and sporting influences

Most English villages have had fetes, club days and sporting matches centred on pubs, and – in the era of male-dominated social activity – the Marsh was no exception. But there were also some interesting variations, with the sport of goalrunning, (a rather sophisticated version of "tag"), for example, being widely practised for the first fifty or so years of the 20th century. Bat-and-trap, an essentially Kentish pastime[10] was also prevalent for a time, before going out of favour and then being revived in Lydd's pubs. Kick-up-jenny, quoits, spinning jenny and the wheel of fortune were more gentle pub pursuits, played particularly in Rye. Also highly popular were cock fighting (even after the activity had been banned) and hare coursing, in which two hounds at a time would be let off to chase a hare across the marshes. After a day tramping around with the dogs, a hot meal and drinks were very welcome and most coursing took place from a country pub. Once again, Romney Marsh had no monopoly on what most would fail to recognise as a sport today, but it was a real centre for that activity. Because it was dependent upon the goodwill and co-operation of local landowners, it had to be highly regulated and organised. The John Jones Coursing Club – named after a JP who was one of the main landowners – met on winter Monday nights during the late 19th and early 20th centuries and was probably the most significant of the various coursing clubs in the area. Most historians are in agreement that only four Marsh venues were sanctioned to host it, but there is dispute as to which these were (confusion is probably due to membership of the coursing clubs not being mutually exclusive). The Black Bull at Newchurch was almost certainly one, as it claimed to be the headquarters of the club and had a photo of its patron hanging prominently in its hall. The provenance of the Star at St Mary-in-the-Marsh is also fairly indisputable as, by hosting the coursing club meeting every Boxing Day, it was allowed to open all day – a very unusual and sought after privilege in years past. Of the others you can perm two from any of the following, which all have strong claims: the Shepherd & Crook (Burmarsh); the Dolphin (Lydd); the Royal Oak (Bonnington); the Star (Lydd); and the Bell (Ivychurch).[11]

A hare coursing event hosted by the Royal William (Old Billy), Camber – not part of the John Jones circuit!

10. Some born over the Sussex border may take exception to this statement.
11. Some newspaper reports of the time state that events at the Bell were part of the John Jones circuit, but these cannot be taken as gospel. However, there was also a very active Lydd & District Coursing Club (in which the Bell and Dolphin featured heavily in the fixture list), which may in part explain this confusion.

Other sporting backdrops include golf; although the area would not now be described as a hotbed of the sport, the Littlestone Golf Club was a major course in its heyday and the *raison d'être* for the development and early success of the Grand (later Pope's) Hotel. At its height, members of royalty and the cabinet would frequently be found on the links at Littlestone, and even now the course stages qualifying competitions for the British Open (when held at nearby Sandwich).

Friendly Societies have also been prevalent on the Marsh. Indeed, there are a number of stories of breweries having to make up shortfalls from funds paid over in good faith for this purpose but misappropriated by landlords who were either greedy or unable to cover their expenses through legitimate means of trade. Today, there are fewer activities centred on pubs. Even the traditional staples of darts and pool are on the wane, although there are others, some of which are on the up. Prominent amongst these are boules (petanque) and quizzes, although even for these there are not the numbers there once were who are prepared to organise and administer. Indeed, the fact that there are healthy crib, dominoes, darts, boules and quiz leagues still operating on the Marsh is down to one of the area's unsung heroes. This a farmer from East Guldeford, Dennis Leeds-George, and in many Marsh pubs you will find his distinctive fixture lists and league tables for one or more of these activities. The single-minded dedication of Dennis has helped pub culture to survive in very difficult economic times.

Railway influences

Three of the larger Marsh drinking establishments were purpose-built to serve the needs of the railway companies that constructed the Hastings to Ashford line (completed in 1851) and the New Romney Branch Line (1881). These were the Railway (Appledore) and the Station Hotels at New Romney and Lydd.[12]

The Railway is the only one to have retained its original name throughout its life, although that sadly closed its doors early in 2013. Indeed, only one of those hotels is currently still trading – that at New Romney. Ironically, this is the only one where the line (its original *raison d'etre*) has been removed! However, this statement may be regarded as slightly disingenuous in that Lydd hosts only one train a week – servicing the Power Station. Also ironic is that the New Romney hotel has managed to cash in on the trade of another line, the Romney, Hythe & Dymchurch Railway (RH&DR), which has its headquarters just across the road. In recognition of this, it changed its name to the Captain Howey (co-founder of the aforementioned light railway) in 1974. Where the Station at Lydd is concerned, its name was later changed to the Bridge Inn to reflect the fact that the only overbridge on the Marsh line was built here.

---

12. Whilst Rye also had a Railway Hotel, this was already established before the advent of the railway (subsequently changing its name to reflect the new transport link).

Railway Heritage: the original Railway Hotel at New Romney (top left) survives, albeit under a new name; whilst at Appledore (top right) the Railway stands boarded up, in 2014 – prior to conversion the following year. At Lydd, the dilapidated Bridge Inn (above, centre) also reflects the fortunes of the railway it once served

Pub names and signs

As far as the names are concerned, many – predictably – relate to the sea. There have been at least four Ships over the years; a Jolly Sailor; two Jolly Fishermans; a Neptune; two Hope & Anchors; a Pilot Inn; and even a Seahorse. And the most popular for Marsh pubs over the years is that of another marine symbol, with no less than six establishments having incorporated the name "Dolphin". This mammal has traditionally been seen by sailors as a friendly creature that would twine itself around a ship's anchor to stop it dragging during a storm.

Although there are a number elsewhere within the south east, surprisingly there is no Smugglers' Inn (notwithstanding that the Ship at Dymchurch was informally known as such for a period and the Britannia at Dungeness bore the name for an even shorter time). There are five pubs going by the name of the Cinque Ports (with very slight variations), reflecting the area's heritage and defence of the realm. The most common pub name in the country is the Red Lion, and at least four establishments on the Marsh have borne this down the years. One of these (at Snargate) is more widely known as "Doris's", in recognition of the remarkable landlady, who was true to her promise to keep the establishment the way it had always been, shunning modern conventions such as electric lighting and inside toilets. Another is that at Hythe, formerly known as the Three Mariners. Nationally, the latter name is not that prevalent, but it has been shared by three other Marsh hostelries, one of which lives on in that rarity of modern drinking culture – a pub that does not rely on food sales.

The pub sign is an often overlooked genre but some very good examples have appeared over the years. As a medium, its profile was much raised by Whitbread in the 1950s. Up until shortly before World War II, few Whitbread pubs displayed inn signs of any note, unless prepared or commissioned by the licensee. However, the company realised that this was a weakness in their branding strategy and accordingly, in 1937, appointed a number artists and designers to their staff. From 1949, in addition to the signs themselves, the company produced several series of 8 by 5 cm miniature reproductions, which were given out to customers and which spawned a collecting craze.

These reproductions, similar to cigarette cards, were initially produced in aluminium (there was a shortage of card post-war) and soon became very popular with collectors. Although Whitbread later extended the boundaries, the first three series were centred on their pubs within Kent and the eastern part of East Sussex, and no less than 11 pubs on the Romney Marsh were so featured.

A selection of the Whitbread reproduction inn signs depicting Marsh pubs. The Three Mariners, The Plough and Botolph's Bridge all featured in series 3 (first issued in 1951)

These miniatures are still sought after today, with collections and individual "cards" fetching high prices on internet auction sites.

Shepherd Neame have also produced some inn signs worthy of comment over the years, although their current policy of replacing existing signs with black and white line drawings has arguably detracted from their appeal.

The changing face of Shepherd Neame pub signs, illustrated by these pictures of the Britannia at Dungeness (above from left, 1988; 2010; and 2013)

These new signs are, however, of very good quality and based on traditional wood-cut designs. The company additionally employs a freehand artist, who signwrites directly onto its pubs' walls without the use of stencils or adhesive vinyls.

An example of the Shepherd Neame signwriter's art (Woolpack, Brookland 2014)

Architecture

It can be imagined that the large number of pubs featured within this book display a wide range of architectural styles, reflecting their age. But something that is more curious is that a number of buildings in the area (particularly those dating from the 1930s) were constructed with "twins" in nearby villages – often mirror images. Where pubs are concerned, it is often quoted that a Ham Street building – the Duke's Head – is a mirror image of the former

Stonebridge Inn at Woodchurch. But not so reported is the similarity between two other pubs featured in this book: the Ship at Lade and Warehorne's World's Wonder.

The Ship (Lade; left) in 2013 and the World's Wonder (Warehorne) in 2014. Both – sadly – have closed recently and the Ship has been demolished to make way for yet more housing. There seems little likelihood of the World's Wonder re-opening as a pub

The changing landscape

Many of the pubs featured in this book are no longer open for business, mirroring the national trend as lamented above. But it is particularly sad when a village loses its only hostelry.

A case in point is Newchurch, where the Black Bull once really did represent the heart of the community. There are some wonderful tales told about this pub, which had a reputation during the 1980s for serving the best (largest!) pub sandwiches in Kent. To many, Newchurch is now only half the place it was.

The basic but wonderful bar of the Black Bull, Newchurch, pictured in the 1940s (picture: courtesy Kent Messenger)

Other villages retain a pub presence, but smaller than previously. Brookland, for example, still has two hostelries although probably its most patronised (the Alliance) has now been closed for over 30 years and been converted to residential use. Appledore once boasted five pubs, but is now down to one. And the coastal settlements of Dungeness, Lade and Greatstone have all hosted pubs that were little more than glorified wooden shacks on the shingle.

Recently, there has been a spate of further closures, some of which threaten to be permanent. Character and community pubs that have closed since 2012 include the Seahorse at Greatstone and the Ship at Lade, with the future of the Star at Lydd very much in limbo. In not all cases does the community have an alternative.

On the credit side, it is gratifying to note that the Plough at New Romney re-opened as a community-run pub in 2013 after eight months of closure.

A selection of pubs that have closed since 2010: (clockwise from top left) The Prince of Wales, New Romney; Star (Lydd); Seahorse (Greatstone); and Ship (Lade)

Iconic pubs

There is clearly a degree of subjectivity in allocating the term "iconic", but there are a number of pubs on the Marsh that stand out as being special. Top of the list must be the Red Lion at Snargate. Its timeless appearance – indeed, its refusal to move with the times – has launched trips from all over the world. Of all the genuine smugglers' pubs on the Marsh, the Woolpack at Brookland is noteworthy for a number of reasons. These include the simplicity of its architecture, its wonderful inglenook fireplace, its smuggling artefacts and the fact that – despite its current distance from the sea – it once served as a beacon keeper's cottage (in effect an early lighthouse). On the current coastline, the Britannia well represents the mood of Dungeness and is also a reminder of those long-gone pubs that formerly also stood on the shingle peninsular. And, if you want a typical English village with just a church, a pub and a few houses, you could do far worse than to seek out St Mary-in-the-Marsh and its Star public house.

A church, a phone box and a pub: classic simplicity to be found at St Mary-in-the Marsh

Landlords and landladies

Traditionally, the role of looking after drinking premises fell for a long time to the female of the species, as reflected in the general term "alewife". But this started to change from the 19th century, with couples increasingly seeing the joint tenure of a pub as a respectable and worthwhile vocation. Pubs often remained in the same families for many years, and many throughout the land have been defined by long-serving or eccentric landlords/landladies. The Marsh is no exception and in the former category, Doris Jemison of Snargate's Red Lion again stands out, the pub having been in her family for over 100 years. But longevity has also been demonstrated by many other Marsh publicans. In the eccentric category, "Flat-cap Sid" of the Warren at New Romney warrants a special mention: he had a pet donkey which he would regularly lead upstairs, as well as a psychotic cat. He was probably what would nowadays be termed bi-polar, and hanged himself in his own pub.

Whilst it has not been unusual in the past for landlords to juggle their responsibilities with other tasks (frequently combining running the pub with village blacksmith duties), the Marsh can also make the unusual claim that two of the names appearing above its pub doors have been those of nationally-known wrestlers. And even more noteworthy is that one landlord, having been convicted of murder, exercised his right to a last request by taking a drink in his own pub en route to the gallows!

Doris Jemison's role as Romney Marsh's longest-serving landlady has been suitably acknowledged through this painting by local artist Brian Oxley. It is part of the mural "Indigenous Romney Marsh" commissioned by the Sainsbury supermarket chain and currently displayed on a long-term basis outside their New Romney store

Haunted pubs

A large number of the Marsh's pubs lay claim to be haunted. Whether you believe in the phenomenon or not, a ghost can be good for business. There are some hostelries where locals genuinely feel that they have experienced a close encounter – which may or may not be linked to the time they have spent there. But, where this is not the case, a landlord may well be tempted to invent one of his own. Again, the history attached to many of the Marsh pubs (and particularly the smuggling trade) lends scope and potential credibility to claims. The Walnut Tree at Aldington is one such, where the sound of muffled shouts and the dragging of a body have been linked to a murder that occurred when smugglers fell out in the 19th century. And at the Warren, there are a number of very credible witnesses who believe that Flat-cap Sid has returned to keep an eye on the place.

More imaginatively, a claim has been made that, of no less than eight categories of haunting at the Rye's Mermaid Inn, one involves a full pitched battle. If you see this one, please let me know and I'll have a pint of whatever you've been drinking.

2

Coastal Villages

For many years, the coastal communities of Romney Marsh have played host to day trippers from London and the southeast, and to holidaymakers from further afield. In the latter category, in addition to those who have patronised the numerous caravan parks dotted around the coast, are many who have flocked to the area's holiday camps. These include the current sites at Romney Sands (formerly Maddiesons) at Greatstone and Pontins, Camber Sands. This tourist trade has helped to shape some of the Marsh's coastal pubs, although others have remained more loyal to the local trade, and many boast a long history – often with smuggling as a common backdrop.

Camber

It is a surprise to many that East Sussex not only has a sandy beach, but in Camber Sands one that – at five miles long and gently shelving – is one of the largest and most child-friendly in the country. This has been instrumental in the development of the area, which is subject to huge seasonal variations in terms of occupancy. Its drinking establishments to an extent reflect this. The only pub that really catered to the local market over any length of time started out serving fishermen and was later additionally patronised by golfers from the nearby Rye Links before relocating into the centre of the village. But it gave up the unequal struggle with market forces and closed around the turn of the 21st century.

Camber Castle, 69 Lydd Road, Camber, TN31 7RS

This is a huge, unpretentious 1970s estate-style pub, with a car park to match. Unkind internet posts have likened it to a warehouse, with the atmosphere of an aircraft hangar. This is unfair, but reflects that it can be very quiet during winter months. It caters primarily for the adjacent Pontins Holiday camp – also acting as the "local" for Pontins staff – and comes alive during the summer, when entertainment is laid on most weekends. In its first decade, it worked hard to cultivate a Mediterranean flavour and in the 1980s had the distinction of being the only Scottish & Newcastle pub on the Marsh.

The upstairs room has been regularly used as a venue for classical music recitals and practice. In recent years, the high parking charges levied by the local council have allowed the Castle to use its own large car park during the day to bring in extra revenue.

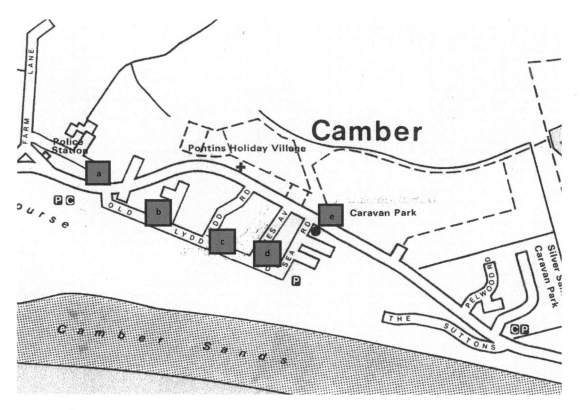

Key to Camber pubs and bars

a – The Gallivant
b – (Green) Owl
c – site of (second) Royal William
d – Dunes Bar
e – Camber Castle

Map of Camber(© Philip's; Reproduced by permission of Ordnance Survey on behalf of HMSO. © Crown copyright 100043101. All rights reserved.)

The Camber Castle, now in the shadow of the Little Cheyne Court Wind Farm

Dunes Bar and Restaurant, Old Lydd Road, Camber, TN31 7RH

In terms of Camber's pubs, the Dunes Bar is very much a newcomer. For much of its life, a single-storey building on this site provided a variety of services of the café/arcade variety. Old photographs (including those currently adorning the bar) depict it as a general store offering a tea room, groceries, provisions and fancy goods (see below).

The Dunes Bar in its previous uses c. 1930

The Dunes Bar, 2013

The current owners saw its potential and converted it to a quality pub and restaurant, which opened in 2005. It is very popular during the spring and summer months and has justifiably been described as having a "classy feel".

(Green) Owl, 11 Old Lydd Road, Camber, TN31 7RE

This small free house and hotel opposite the sand dunes has at various times served as a tea rooms, post office and stores. It has gone by various names, including the Camber Café and the Tunbridge Stores (it stands on the corner of Tunbridge Road). The Green Owl first became a hotel/restaurant in the late 1960s, and by 1983 had become a free house. There is no particular significance in the name, which was taken from that of a local house, although the interior now sports a vast collection of ornamental owls. After complete refurbishment in 1987 the restaurant was increased to seat 24 diners and bow windows were added. It has thrived by catering to a number of different markets: in the summer it caters to a niche market, specialising in golfing and bird watching holidays, and its restaurant is so popular that prospective diners have to be turned away. But in the winter months it becomes a popular and comfortable locals' pub. The Green prefix was dropped at the end of 2015.

The Gallivant, New Lydd Road, Camber, TN31 7RB

This started life in the 1960s, as the Blue Dolphin Motel (one of a number of establishments in the area to have traded similarly). Later it changed its name to The Place; the less than convincing reason given for its change to the current name in September 2010 was that some people found The Place gave a confusing impression. Regardless of its name, the establishment has developed something of a cult status in recent years, having been reviewed very

Structurally, the Owl has changed little from the 1930s (top left) to the current day (2012, top right). However, an earlier photo (left) shows it as a single-storey building

favourably by a number of the quality national newspapers. These have described its ambience as "shabby chic coastal", although its owners prefer the term "New England style". In addition to 18 bedrooms, it offers a beach bistro with a bleached wood bar. This is open to the public and serves food that has been recommended in the *Michelin Guide*.

The Gallivant, pictured in 2014

Royal William/"Old Billy" (1), Lydd Road, Camber, TN31 7QS

There has been a lot that is incorrect written about the "Old Billy". Misunderstanding seems to arise from the fact that it has existed on two different sites. For the greater part of its life, it was situated on the north side of the Lydd–Rye road. It initially served the needs not only of Camber residents, but those of fishermen from nearby Rye Harbour. The original building was constructed around 1807 by William Morris, a former ship's carpenter. Morris had plied much of his trade aboard the sloop the *Royal William*, and it was for sentimental reasons that, on leaving the service and setting up home in Camber, he bestowed this name upon his pub. The first inn sign, which dominated this modest wooden building, was an elaborate model ship, which he himself carved. This sign became a talking point and was in place for many years. When Morris died, it disappeared, only to turn up many years later in a London auction house.[1] Being additionally a known meeting place for smugglers, there were times when the building could not cope with its volume of customers. On such occasions, the primitive wall between the saloon and public bars would be pulled back to create more room. This really could be a lively hostelry at times, and it was no coincidence that it became a regular haunt for the press gang, up until as late as the 1860s.

The original Royal William – still sporting William Morris's carved ship – pictured (probably) in the late 1890s

With the opening of the golf links in 1894, the Old Billy took on a new lease of life, together with a more upmarket clientele. Unfortunately, however, it burned down in 1900, only to re-emerge some seven years later. An unusual claim to fame in its new guise was that one of the competitors in the famed 1914 Air Race from London to Paris (Mr Louis Noel),

---

1. It was sold to an American dealer and, unfortunately, shipped to the United States, never to be heard of since.

The current golf club building (providing quarters for the staff, right) is quite recognisable as the Royal William rebuilt on the original site (pictured, left, in 1925)

having run into trouble, ditched his plane on the English shore and walked to the Royal William where he calmly ordered breakfast!

Although becoming a regular venue for the Rye and East Guldeford Hare Coursing Club, it does seem that the Old Billy was fated, as another fire some 30 years after the first caused further significant damage. The site was then purchased by the Rye Golf Club and the building restored.

Royal William/"Old Billy" (2), Old Lydd Road, Camber, TN31 7RH

The new Royal William went up in 1936/37 at the corner of Old Lydd Road and Lydd Road, but was soon commandeered by the army to serve as a canteen for the duration of WWII. It was rebuilt very soon after, with a design that – like the Jolly Fisherman at Greatstone –

The sign outside the flats (bottom right) and some design similarities give clues to the location of the second Royal William pub (left, pictured in the 1960s)

resembled a ship. Its beachside location was a huge draw, and the new pub was hugely successful and popular during the 1960s, tapping into the holiday camp trade. It also had an impressive function room, which hosted numerous wedding receptions throughout the 1970s.

Unfortunately, a pub of this size has huge overheads and these proved unsustainable outside the holiday months. It limped through the latter years of the 20th century, but after years of neglect and disuse, planning permission was granted in October 2005 for demolition of the pub and erection of 19 dwellings and a café.

Dungeness

Dungeness does not just have a huge shingle beach; it is *all* shingle. It is the largest such expanse in Europe, and has a unique habitat supporting a surprisingly diverse range of flora and fauna. The landscape can be both bleak and inspiring – particularly with its surreal backdrop of nuclear power stations – but the number of dwellings is very low. Far from being a well-kept secret, however, the 'Ness has now been well and truly "discovered" by the media. This has had much to do with the late film director Derek Jarman, who fell in love with the place and spent his last few years there. His distinctive black, yellow-framed bungalow with its spectacular garden has been preserved by his partner, and still draws tourists from all over the world.

The boundaries of Dungeness are difficult to establish and have not appeared consistently on maps over time. The northern edge is quite clearly defined by the entry sign to the Dungeness estate, but to the south west there is less clarity. Within this narrative I have included the former hamlet of Galloways, some two or three miles from the headland. The settlement is long gone and, whilst it was geographically closer to Lydd, the topography is identical to that of the rest of the Ness.

Right up until the late 1950s, a specially designed beach cart (a wide-wheeled horse drawn cart) was used to deliver beer to the Brittania from Style & Winch and to return the empty barrels, whilst boxes of fish were delivered on a sledge with runners made of local staves. This cart has been preserved and is currently exhibited in Lydd Museum

To many, Dungeness epitomises the splendour and remoteness of Romney Marsh, and there could be little more itypical of this than pubs of basic wooden construction on the shingle itself. At one time, Dungeness boasted at least three such establishments. Whilst the Britannia remains (albeit in a much altered guise), the British Sailor and the Hope & Anchor are sadly defunct. Other similar places may have existed as beerhouses, but there are unfortunately gaps in local records and histories.

Fishing is an activity that has been synonymous with Dungeness, and a small number of families have trawled the seas here for generations. Prominent amongst these have been the Oillers, Tarts, Richardsons and Freathys. Traditionally, these families have additionally taken on coastguard and lifeboat roles, so it is interesting to note that some of these names also appear as pub licensees.

Britannia Inn, Dungeness Road, Dungeness, TN29 9ND

This single storey pub is of unusual appearance, but quite in keeping with both its location on the shingle of Dungeness and its history. Originally a simple beerhouse constructed in 1850, it has led a chequered existence. The original name may have been the British Inn (it was certainly known as such throughout the early 20th century), and it was significantly redesigned in 1926. 1930s photographs show an austere building, which appears to be comprised largely of corrugated iron. During WWII, an emplacement for machine guns was installed opposite the pub and, whilst there is no evidence of enemy aircraft being shot down, a British plane did crash land here in 1940/41. Its subsequent reclamation by the RAF was watched from the pub by a large crowd. At times it has been known locally as the Black Pig.

Soon after the war, this building was replaced nearby with a more solid structure on the site of either (depending on your source) two air-raid shelters (bunkers), or two former barrack rooms. At this time it was still known as the British Inn, but this building in turn perished in a fire in 1952. The current brick building was completed in 1955, and named the

The British Inn in the 1930s (picture: courtesy Kent Messenger)

Britannia. The concrete floor of the new pub provided one of the few even surfaces on the 'Ness. Accordingly, it was very attractive to local children, who wished to take part in the latest craze of roller-skating and who would break in on a regular basis.

The Britannia has since enjoyed mixed fortunes, although prospering in the early 1980s when barbecues were held on Saturday evenings throughout the summer. It was also the hub of the popular Dungeness May Day parade and fun day (which generally descended into endless forays between it and the Pilot!). After changing its name to The Smugglers, it closed in 1992.

The Britannia – in need of decoration – in 1988

After it had been sold, however, the new owners breathed fresh life into it and secured the approval of locals by reverting to the name of The Britannia. In the 21st century it has secured a reputation for good food and trades on its location as the "only pub in Dungeness". This is a clearly a sideswipe at the nearby Pilot Inn: whilst the Pilot has itself tried to cash in on increasing media interest in the unique landscape and culture of Dungeness, it currently sits just the other side of the border with Lydd-on-sea. The Britannia has featured in a number of television shows – most notably a 2006 episode of the Inspector Lindley series[2] and a 2007 instalment of *EastEnders* (which centred around the pub). It also lends its name to the adjacent points on the RH&DR, which enable trains to access the turning loop.

British Sailor

Part of the former hamlet of Galloways, the British Sailor stood at the end of Galloways Road, which was realigned when the army came to Lydd. The site is, accordingly, now to be found at the end of the private army track that leads from Tourney Road to the sea.

---

2. Entitled *Natural Causes.*

The Britannia in 2013

Historians believe that the building was initially a cottage for coastguards stationed here, probably dating from around 1832. Directories confirm that it was certainly trading as a beerhouse in 1855, largely for the benefit of Rye fishermen, who would call in on their way home.

In 1914, the pub was advertising Sunday roasts (served with a sweet) at the cost of 4d. This – a pub selling substantial meals – was unusual for the time, although the inhabitants of Dungeness have, out of circumstance, for long ploughed their own furrow.

Photographs taken before the outbreak of WWII show an unpretentious wooden building, which was home to the Freathys and other local fishermen, with one room used as a bar. Other 20th century landlords included Charles Oiller. But trade ceased in 1938 and the pub never re-opened. The building was allowed to decay and, although remaining in place for a number of years, was fully demolished in the 1960s. Parts of the foundations can sometimes still be seen on the beach, although only when exposed by violent wave action.

The British Sailor, c. 1936

Dover Hoveller

Little can be confirmed of the Dover Hoveller, except that it features in smuggling folklore and is listed in a directory of 1818. Suggestions have been made that it was the early name used for the Pilot,[3] but it is more likely that it was a discrete building, probably situated to the south (close to the site of the 1961 lighthouse). It was probably no more than a basic wooden shack serving as an alehouse. "Hoveller" was the name given to an unlicensed pilot who would watch the sea from an improvised shelter, commonly an upturned boat. His main purpose was to identify vessels in distress and provide assistance for a fee. In reality, however, some hovellers were rather opportunists or were even involved in the dark practice of wrecking.

Hope & Anchor, Dengemarsh

In the area of Pen Bars (which is still marked on some maps), the Hope & Anchor was sited at the end of Dengemarsh Road, which is still just about negotiable from Lydd – at the cost of some discomfort if travelling by car. In an isolated community like Dungeness, arrangements at establishments such as the Hope & Anchor and the British Sailor were largely informal, irregular and *ad hoc*. Luxury was not a prerequisite for pubs of this type, which we would not recognise as such today. We know that the Hope & Anchor was trading in 1847, and was acquired by Finn's Brewery in 1879. At this time it was a tumbledown, tarred and weatherboarded timber-built bungalow comprising four bedrooms, a sitting room and large living room, surrounded by similar (but smaller) fishermen's huts. Reports from the early 20th century suggest that there was no proper bar area as such; and only a bench and a few scattered chairs provided creature comforts. The smell of stale tobacco and old ale dominated, when not masked by the by-products of the frying and boiling of local fish – often supplied by its customers. In addition to Rye fishermen, who also used the British Sailor, the Hope & Anchor was host to French and Dutch pilots, and tales would be exchanged by the light of an old oil lamp. Records show that Richard Tart was the landlord in 1938, and almost certainly its last one. The pub achieved wider exposure during the war (in 1944) when several of the Allied leaders – including Winston Churchill – gathered there to watch experiments with a new flame thrower, tested on an old coastguard station nearby. The Hope & Anchor was – or at least some of its patrons were – unquestionably mixed up with smuggling and in 1888 the landlord was fined after being found in possession of contraband tobacco and cigars. Similarly, the post-war story is still told of a stranger who called there, quaffed a pint of ale and struck up a wide-ranging conversation with its other customers. He then locked the door, announced that he was a Customs Officer, and began a search for contraband. He had almost certainly been tipped off about smuggling and, after a thorough search (which included the contents of pans boiling on the stove!), found packets of tobacco hidden behind pictures on

---

3. See separate entry under Lydd-on-sea. The Pilot has existed on more than one site; and the similarity of meaning (hoveller/pilot) lends credence to this alternative.

The Hope & Anchor around the end of the 1920s

the wall. The upshot was that the landlord was heavily fined. This incident can be dated fairly accurately, as the pub closed in 1947. By 1955, the building was a crumbling shambles and soon after all traces had disappeared. Some sources have claimed that its site lies under the power station, but – although nearby – this would not appear to be the case.

Jolly Sailor, Dungeness

Even less is known of the Jolly Sailor than of the Dover Hoveller. It, too, was listed in the 1818 directory. As for the Hoveller, numerous theories have been put forward. Suggestions have been made that it too was a former name of the Pilot (trading as such up until 1832); that it may have been adjacent to the Pilot; or even that it was a predecessor of the British Sailor.

Dymchurch

Dymchurch today is a rather unremarkable seaside village, bustling with holidaymakers in the season and quiet in the winter. But it is steeped in history and Dymchurch Wall has for long been the key to holding the sea at bay and ensuring that the Marsh has not been reclaimed. Because of the need for prompt decisions to be made in the event of flooding, Henry III granted a Royal Charter giving the right of self-government, with unique Administrative and Judicial powers, which were at the outset vested in the 23 Lords of the Manors of Romney Marsh.[4] The Lords of the Manor have frequently held their meetings at the Dymchurch courthouse.

---

4. The powers of the Lords were eroded by subsequent Government legislation, although the Lords still meet annually to hold the Grand Lathe.

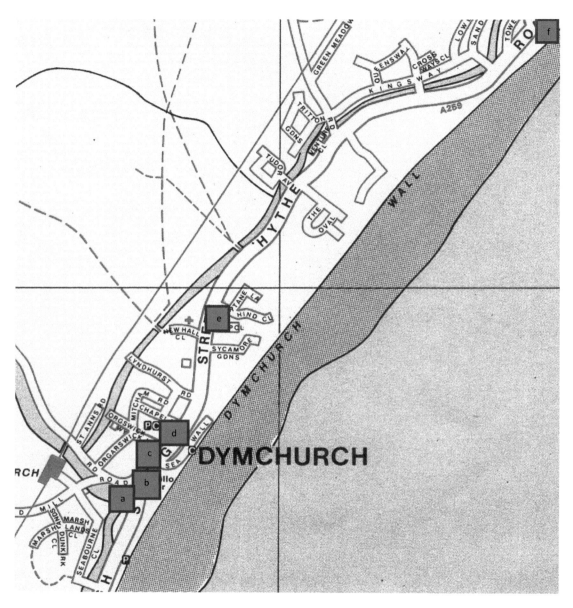

Key to Dymchurch pubs

a – site of second Rose Inn   b – Ocean (Victoria) Inn

c – site of first Rose Inn   d – City of London

e – The Ship Inn   f – Neptune Inn

Map of Dymchurch © Philip's; Reproduced by permission of Ordnance Survey on behalf of HMSO. © Crown copyright 100043101. All rights reserved.)

Dymchurch has been patronised by and features in works by writers as diverse as Rudyard Kipling (whose celebrated poem *The Smuggler's Song* makes specific reference to Dymchurch Wall), Richard Barham, Ford Madox Hueffer (Ford) and John Davison. But the most well-known of Dymchurch's writers must be Russell Thorndike, whose *Doctor Syn* saga created a legend. Thorndike was very well acquainted with the pubs of Dymchurch, and they feature widely within the Syn novels. The Thorndike family were part of a quite extraordinary literary and art set that met up in Dymchurch most weekends in the summer months – and which heartily enjoyed its hostelries! Dymchurch continues to host a Day of Syn (a rather misleading title as it spans the whole August Bank Holiday weekend!) in alternate years.

It is pleasing (at least to this author) that a village the size of Dymchurch still supports four pubs. In addition to those pubs listed below, Dymchurch was also home to a 1934 building that at various times was known as the **Silver Casino**, the **Martello Beach Hotel** and the **Seaborne Club**.[5] It is believed that – at least for part of its hotel existence – this had a bar open to the public. It was demolished in 1963.

City of London, 68–70 High Street, Dymchurch, TN29 0NL

A selection of City of London inn signs. Left to right: 1951 Whitbread reproduction; 2012; and 2013

Dating back to the 16th century, this former coaching house has a long history. Legend has it that the pub was originally named the Sea Wall Tavern, changing its name after the *City of London* brig was wrecked on the Dymchurch Wall, and the pub's owner killed in trying to effect rescue of the ship's crew. This has been reported as fact in a number of guidebooks. The story, however, is fictional and comes from Thorndike (the episode appearing in *Doctor*

---

5.   Pub names given in bold are those that do not have their own entry in the book.

Syn Returns, the second volume of the Syn saga). It is likely that the name was taken from a tug that regularly worked in the English Channel, although Whitbread have claimed that it relates to an ancient charter granted by Edward VI.

Although it is The Ship that is the most frequently mentioned Dymchurch pub within the Syn novels, the City of London makes frequent appearances – and in real life was the favourite haunt of another author and playwright, Noel Coward. The City of London was itself highly involved in the free trade, and it is rumoured that the remains of a smuggler – fatally wounded in an exchange with revenue officers – are secreted within one of its walls. The pub was extended in 1928 when the stables were converted into an office and bar, with the adjacent forge also incorporated (providing a further bar). Prior to this, the landlord had additionally been the village blacksmith. Whilst not an unusual state of affairs across the country, there is no other record of any other Marsh landlord performing this dual function.

The changing faces of Dymchurch's City of London. Clockwise from top left: c. 1905; 2011; and 2013

In the 1980s, reflecting the rather questionable taste of the decade (and in common with the Bahia Bar at nearby St Mary's Bay), the City of London boasted a Spanish Bar. Mercifully, this was a short-lived experiment. Struggling financially, the pub unfortunately closed for a short time in 2010, before re-opening a few months later as a Sports Bar.

The signboard hanging outside the inn has at various times depicted the arms of the City of London, which incorporates Wat Tyler's[6] dagger. In 2013, the pub underwent a comprehensive makeover, which has led to the incorporation of the Seawall Tavern name. Whilst most pub lovers are not in favour of name changing, this nod to local legend has been welcomed (and the City of London name remains more prominent – as shown).

Neptune Inn, 127–128 Hythe Road, Dymchurch, TN29 0TS

Despite its postal address, this pub is significantly to the north of Dymchurch village, and halfway to Hythe. The somewhat remote location meant that it was at one time a popular meeting place for smugglers and used for the hiding and storage of contraband.

The Neptune pictured in 2013

The historic 14th century building was originally a farmhouse, subsequently becoming a coaching inn. However, it has served many other purposes over the years. At one time it housed monks who were stationed there by the Archbishop of Canterbury to work on drainage and reclamation of a large area of Romney Marsh, and at others is has served as two separate cottages; a tea rooms; and the Mac Erin Guest House. In the 1980s it was a motel and chalet offering half-board accommodation and regularly hosting cabaret nights.

The Neptune underwent extensive renovation in 1999–2000, and an extension housing a restaurant to the side (which has detracted a little from its aesthetic appearance) added in

---

6. Wat Tyler was a man of Kent who in 1381 led an armed revolt against an early poll tax. In a meeting between the rebels and the Lord Mayor of London, the latter stabbed Wat Tyler to death.

2013. The large car park is a good indication of its reliance on passing trade (inevitable, given its location), although it also caters for patrons of the adjacent caravan site. It was subject to a further comprehensive refurbishment at the start of 2015.

Ocean Inn, 2 High Street, Dymchurch, TN29 0NG

Built in the 18th century (both 1733 and 1783 are dates regularly suggested), this pub became part of the Finn empire in 1886. At some point it changed its name to the Victoria: the likelihood is that this would have coincided with Queen Victoria's golden jubilee in 1887; although it could alternatively have marked her diamond jubilee ten years later or her death in 1901.

Most sources agree that the original name (the Ocean Inn) was only discovered by the landlord after some extensive renovations undertaken post-WWII, although this would smack of collective amnesia. After all, Thorndike refers to it by its original name in a 1935 novel, so this would suggest that its history was quite widely known. Two dates are again generally favoured for its reversion to the Ocean – this time 1949 and 1958 – which is puzzling, as drainage rent records show that the change occurred in 1952–53. But it is still known colloquially by some older regulars as "The Vic".

What is not disputed is that for a long period the pub was one of those Marsh hostelries defined by the longevity of its custodians. In this case, it was popular landlady, Mrs Swift, who by 1921 had clocked up 45 years' service. Also typical of Marsh pubs is the Ocean's involvement in the smuggling trade. Inside can be found some impressive murals depicting smuggling scenes. These date back a significant time, but have recently been restored. The pub, reputedly haunted by a mischievous ghost, is very lively in the summer months and its close proximity to the beach is a huge selling point.

The Ocean has always involved itself in the community and in the 1960s staged an annual Guy Fawkes pageant. Nowadays, it features prominently in the Day of Syn revels – which include the staging of a firing squad "execution" in the pub garden. An even more macabre incident that involves the Ocean is recalled by Vic Haisell in his book *St Mary's Bay – The Story*

The Victoria (1930s – left) and Ocean Inn (2012 – right)

of a Seaside Village. In 1947, a resident of St Mary's Bay and her daughter had been shot dead by the woman's lover, who then turned the gun on himself. Later on, in the Ocean (the Victoria at the time of the incident), the Dymchurch Mortuary attendant overheard a couple arguing over the appearance and size of the dead man. The attendant settled the argument by saying: "he was the same size as me. I'm wearing his suit!"

Rose Inn (two High Street sites)

The least known of all Dymchurch's hostelries, the Rose Inn was recorded in the 18th century, with trade directories listing it as a beerhouse from 1793 (although it may have had an even earlier incarnation as a beerhouse or off licence). The original building, 2 Rose Cottages (opposite Martello Tower no. 24) survives and sports a plaque commemorating the fact that it was later (1921–25) the home of artist Paul Nash. It closed as a pub in 1817 and became a private dwelling. Colin Walker of the Dymchurch Heritage Group has researched its history and concluded that this was probably because the landlord moved to the Ship.

However, the Rose re-opened on a new High Street site (opposite another Martello Tower – no. 25), that now occupied by Tesco Express. The first date that it re-appears in local records is 1843, although it may have significantly pre-dated this. It disappears from records in 1867, and, although this may reflect gaps in local records, it probably did not trade for much longer afterwards.

Some sources additionally suggest that there may have been a Rose & Crown in the village; however, this would seem to stem from an erroneous 18th century census recording of the Rose (the address confirming this).

Rose Cottages c. 1900 (photo courtesy Colin Walker) and 2014

The Ship Inn, 118 High Street, Dymchurch, TN29 0NS

The Ship Inn unashamedly markets itself as the home of Doctor Syn. In point of fact, it was more the home of Syn's factotum, Didimus Mipps. But the seven *Dr Syn* novels feature the pub heavily, and the Ship was certainly the spiritual and second home of Thorndike himself.

The Ship claims to date back to the 16th century, yet there is reference to an inn on this site within a survey undertaken in 1452. The earliest title deeds that can be traced date it to 1618. It would be disappointing if a pub with such strong fictional links to smuggling did not have a *bona fide* link with the free trade, and there is plenty of evidence to confirm its involvement. By virtue of its long sandy beaches and its proximity to the continent, Dymchurch has always been a natural landing place for goods and the Ship was well placed to take full advantage. Indeed, for a time it was informally known as the *Smugglers Inn* (and some histories refer to it as such).

These photos of The Ship show the original (left 1910) and the current (right 2012 – following road realignment) front entrances

Various renovation works over the years have identified a recess within a chimney breast, a sliding wall panel and other places of concealment. It is reliably claimed that there was once also a tunnel connecting it to the nearby church. One of the most intriguing features of the pub is that it appears to have been built back to front, in that it backs on to the main road. Within Dymchurch, the pub is not unique in this: the construction of the new coast road around the turn of the 19th century cut the village in two; the original road from Hythe ran right under the sea wall, into the forecourt of The Ship and then back along the sea wall. At this time the Ship was very much the largest inn/hotel in the area and offered many additional services, such as open and closed carriages for hire, a charabanc service to New Romney and Hythe, a bowling green, quoits and a lawn tennis court. As was the practice of the day, being the foremost pub in the area, it was also used to hold coroner's courts. Despite its prominence and standing, The Ship also offered camping within its field in the 1920s. Internally, significant renovations and extensions were undertaken in 1921 and 1966, the latter involving construction of a new kitchen and dining room to seat 30 diners. In common with the Ocean Inn, The Ship had its own long-serving landlady, with popular licensee Mrs Dorothy Saunders (who was a close friend of Russell Thorndike) running the pub between 1927 and 1965. The pub today sports a number of interesting features, including an attractive staircase and, in one bedroom, an iron ceiling from an 18th century Wealden ironworks. There is much Doctor Syn memorabilia (photographs, paintings and film posters) on display and a selection of related merchandise has been sold at various times. The pub sign itself depicts an image of Dr Syn, hanging from a replica gallows. This not only relates to the gallows tree featured in the Syn novels, but is a reminder that the Dymchurch gallows once stood very close by – on the site of the war memorial, next to the church and opposite the pub. The Ship unfortunately closed in 2016, but was sold on and is due to re-open in 2017.

The Ship Inn sign, across the road from the site of the village gallows

Greatstone-on-sea

The development of Greatstone as a seaside resort makes an interesting story, and is worthy of a small volume of its own. Geographically, even as recently as 1816, the majority of the village as we now know it was still part of Romney Bay, and partly submerged at high tide. But from then onwards shingle started to migrate south and form a barrier, and the reclamation process was accelerated with the building of a sea wall in 1839 and further strengthening in 1900.

Even so, development was very sparse up until the 1920s, when an entrepreneur bought up much of the land, and offered building plots for sale. A great future was predicted for Greatstone as well as neighbouring Littlestone and, in the 1930s, a village plan was drawn up, which had the junction of Coast Road (the Parade) and Dunes Road at its hub. At around the same time Maddieson's Holiday Camp, one of the first in the country, opened its doors at the southern end of the village.

The Southern Railway even diverted its route to try and capitalise on the holiday camp trade and proposed developments. This was in 1937. But, despite the success of the former the reality failed to match the expectations and, although much infilling took place in the

1960s and 1970s, Greatstone remains a fairly quiet seaside resort. However, in the height of the summer, its fine sandy beach remains a huge draw, and its gently shelving nature means that it offers very safe swimming. It is also a prime location for both land yachting and kite-surfing enthusiasts.

The standard-gauge railway is long closed, although much of the old bed track is still clearly visible and can be walked; and, whilst the former Greatstone Dunes station also closed in 1983, the RH&DR nevertheless can still claim the only station still serving the village. This is at the holiday camp – now "rebadged" as Romney Sands.

The village has hosted a number of pubs over the years, two of which shared the same name. Another closed in 2013, but the village still retains two pubs (albeit one that mainly caters to the holiday camp) and a wine bar.

Jolly Fisherman (1), Greatstone

The original Jolly Fisherman was some two miles to the south of the current pub of this name, to the west of Leonard Road (near its junction with Hull Road). A number of buildings are believed to have existed on this site at various times, and it is possible that the first ale-house here was as early as the mid-16th century.

Photographs of the pub at the start of the 20th century show it to have been a basic, timber built structure, very similar to those at the time on the beach at Dungeness. It was then owned by Style & Winch, who closed it in 1935 when they transferred the licence to the site at the Parade (see below). Today, there is nothing to mark its site.

The first Jolly Fisherman pub, pictured very shortly before closure. Its sign lived on for a time, hanging outside the Red House in Madeira Road, Littlestone. This was the residence of the then Bailiff of Romney Marsh, Major Teichman Derville, himself a keen fisherman, seen standing alongside the sign (Picture: courtesy Kent Messenger)

Jolly Fisherman (2), The Parade, Greatstone, TN28 8ST

This art deco pub, built just before WWII, dominates the junction of Dunes Road and The Parade. It is quite incongruous and out of keeping with the rest of the village, but it is a powerful reminder of the fact that Greatstone once had a grand future mapped out.

The "new" Jolly Fisherman (left) pictured just after opening (and only a few months after the photo of its predecessor was taken – see previous page). The picture on the right is from 2013, prior to yet another makeover. Note that the doors on the upper deck have been removed

The building was commissioned by brewers Style and Winch in 1935, as a pub and hotel – to form part of the major development scheme for Greatstone. The original intention was to name it The Ship, as it was designed to resemble a sea-going vessel (although not totally convincing, there are arguably similarities to the bridge of a ship). However, at the last minute Style & Winch (who also owned the original Jolly Fisherman) – realised that there was limited mileage in trying to run two pubs in the same community and decided to close the existing pub and transfer both the licence and the name to the other end of Greatstone. This decision also avoided any possible confusion with the Ship at Lade.

A grand opening was held, with many dignitaries in attendance. These included Councillor C.E. Andrews (who owned and developed the Greatstone estate), the mayor of New Romney and Colonel G.B. Winch (one of the Style & Winch Directors). Referred to in a lavish advertising brochure as a "country hotel", the new Jolly Fisherman had a long saloon bar with a circular window and a second extensive bar leading to rooms on the ground floor. The first floor boasted:

> delightful balconies overlooking the dunes and giving fine views of the English Channel. On each side of the corridor, there are 12 single and double bedrooms each with hot and cold running water.

There was additionally a large tea lounge, above which was a roof garden – providing even better views. The building is little changed today, but the doors and railings on the balcony – clearly visible in postcards of the time – have gone. When war broke out soon after, the pub was requisitioned by the army and – when PLUTO[7] was established – became the officers' mess for the project.

The Jolly Fisherman has struggled financially over the years – hardly surprising given its size and associated overheads and only a relatively small local population outside the holiday season.

Romney Tavern, The Parade, Greatstone, TN28 8RN

This has for long been the bar for residents of the holiday village, which started life as Maddieson's Littlestone Holiday Camp in the late 1920s.

The Romney Tavern in 2013

The Maddieson's bar was a private one for many years, and not always located on the same part of the site. For much of its early life it was known as the Mermaid Bar, but for a period prior to Maddieson's closing in 1980 was the Tavern Bar. By this time it was in the same spot as now (next to the road), and was catering to all – guests, visitors and locals alike. It is justifiably proud of its fine sea views and is very convenient for the beach, and in particular for land yachting devotees.

Seahorse, 109–111 Coast Drive, Greatstone, TN28 8NR

This 1930s building was one of a number in Greatstone constructed with a distinctive green roof. Photographs show that it started off serving teas and refreshments and at some point did service as a general store. It was not until 1970 that it made its debut as a pub, and its

---

7. PLUTO (Pipeline Under the Ocean) was the top-secret project to transport oil across the English Channel to allied forces in France. One of the two major pipelines ran from Walton-on-Thames to Greatstone and Dungeness.

The Seahorse in 1970 (left) and 2013 (post-closure)

golden years were very much in the 70s and 80s, when regular live music made it a popular venue with the younger generation, although it shunned the move to real ale until the mid-1980s. Adverts claiming that it "opens directly onto the beach and offers views over the beach and Channel" were stretching the truth somewhat, as a large shingle car park had to be negotiated prior to reaching the shore.

In 2013 the pub closed, against a backdrop of a vitriolic war of words between the licensee and the landlord, Enterprise Inns, waged through the medium of the local newspaper. But the writing had been on the wall for some time, and in 2014 the pub was converted to private accommodation.

Sotirio's 103 Restaurant, 103 Coast Drive, Greatstone, TN28 8NR

Costas Sotirio took over what was once the Nelson's Head in Hythe (see Chapter 4) in the 1980s, running it as Sotirio's Restaurant. Constrained, however, by the size of the building (which could only seat 60–70 diners), he sought a larger venue. The former Tony's Restaurant at Greatstone (just a couple of doors down from the Seahorse) had been succeeded by **Sonny's Restaurant and Cabaret Bar**, a short-lived enterprise, which closed in 2011. But the

Sotirio's 103 pictured in 2013, some 10 months after opening

premises could accommodate up to 130 and offered the ideal opportunity to Sotirio, who moved his operation here lock, stock and barrel in February 2013. All his staff (including the head chef of 25 years) followed him. Sotirio's has an entertainment licence and offers regular cabaret. Most significantly – in terms of qualification for inclusion in this book! – it has a separate wine and tapas bar upstairs, with a rooftop terrace.

Lade

Lade – adjacent to and north of Lydd-on-Sea, and to the south of Greatstone – is a very small settlement, comprising a few houses and a small parade of shops. It formerly had its own station on the RH&DR, although this soon became downgraded to a halt and disappeared from the timetable in 1977. Lade has only hosted the one pub, albeit on two different but adjacent sites and now sadly closed. This was situated in Taylor Road, a quiet backwater with a few small shops but used by walkers making for the historic Greatstone sound mirrors.

Ship Inn, 13 Taylor Road, Lade, TN29 9PA

The Ship was originally a beerhouse, and a building fairly typical of the area: a no-nonsense single-storey fishermen's dwelling/pub with three bedrooms, a sitting room, a large room for the public and a wooden outside closet. It is unclear when it was first constructed, but records show a member of one of the local fishing families – the Oillers – as being the tenant from 1880 to 1920, when Finn & Sons of Lydd acquired the property.

In 1935, a new building of Dutch Barn design was constructed close to the original, which was demolished soon after. Some remnants of the foundations of the original are still visible, although hard to find.

Lade is not a large community, and has never been a big tourist target. Accordingly, the size of the new premises was always optimistic, and for a long time the Ship – very much a "locals'" pub – struggled to survive. It finally gave up this unequal struggle, and closed its doors in 2010. Shepway District Council refused an application to demolish the pub and construct four houses on the site in 2012/13, on the grounds that the applicant had not demonstrated that the business was unviable. But another application in 2014 was successful.

Littlestone

Like Greatstone, Littlestone was something of a late developer, although it had a head start on its neighbour. The vision of surveyor Henry Tubbs and his solicitor Sir Robert Perks – who had just completed reconstruction of the Hong Kong & Shanghai Railway and was looking for a new project – was behind its development in the 1880s. Together the two men drew up plans for a new seaside resort, which began with the building of an imposing terrace of

The Ship at Lade in 1920 (top); the subsequent building in prosperous times (above left, 1980); and after closure, in 2013

four-storey Victorian houses overlooking the sea, and the splendid Grand Hotel. However, the jewel in their crown was undoubtedly the Littlestone Golf Course, which was laid down in 1888. The Golf Club was to become the focus for the good and the great from all walks of life, and would count many politicians amongst its membership. These included Herbert Asquith and Arthur Balfour (respectively prime minister and leader of the opposition of the day). Some bought their own properties here and notable show-business people were also attracted to the area. However, plans for future development, including a pier and continental ferry terminal, were over-ambitious and – as at Greatstone – failed to come to fruition.

It is clear that Littlestone has always favoured hotels with bars rather than the more traditional English pub. In addition to those listed below, there was also the **Windacre Hotel**, a popular but short-lived venture in the 1980s. This was located in Madeira Road.

Captain Howey (Station Hotel), 1 Littlestone Road, New Romney, TN28 8LN

Completed in 1884 at the New Romney terminus of the new branch line, the Station Hotel was one of three purpose-built railway hotels on the Marsh (the others being at Lydd and Appledore), and was a relatively grand affair. At this time it had stabling attached and served the many weekend visitors to the coast and the Littlestone Golf Club. With the opening of the RH&DR, the Station Hotel was in the unusual, if not unique, position of serving two stations on different

The Station Hotel in the early 20th century (left); and the Captain Howey pictured in 2013

gauge railways. As the main-line traffic decreased, patronage of the RH&DR grew and the Station Hotel came to rely increasingly on custom from that source. Additionally, a number of RH&DR staff took to using it after work. With the closure of the branch line in 1967 and the death of Captain Jack Howey (one of the founders of the RH&DR), it was unsurprising that the establishment was renamed in the latter's honour in 1974.

During the 1990s, the Captain Howey enjoyed something of a cult status, with customers travelling significant distances to enjoy its Sunday night jazz sessions.

Dormy House Hotel, Marine Parade, Littlestone, TN28 8QL

Under plans for development of the new resort of Littlestone this was designated as a hotel, but appears to have operated early on as a private club. It post-dates the Grand/Popes (see below), but by 1930 was in direct and fierce competition with it.

In the 1950s and 1960s it was widely patronised by those using Ferryfield (Lydd) Airport, which it featured on its own postcards. The Dormy House also painted its name on the building's roof. Although this was patently advertising, the owners dressed it up as "a friendly aid to pilots".

A Dormy House postcard from the late 1950s (left) and the building – still recognisable – in current usage (2015)

This apparently wintry photograph was taken on Easter Day 1983, clearly showing the fire damage to the Dormy Hotel inflicted earlier in the year (photo copyright John Baker and licensed for reuse under a Creative Commons Licence)

A popular venue for entertainment, dinner dances were still being staged on a weekly basis well into the 1970s. But the growth of affordable overseas travel ate into the Dormy's core market, and business waned through the decade. When a fire badly damaged the property in February 1983, the hotel closed for good. The building is still recognisable today, despite having been converted into flats.

Grand Hotel (Pope's), The Avenue (Station Road), Littlestone, TN28 8NT

The Grand Hotel was completed in 1891, to cater for visitors (mostly from London) keen to take on the challenge of the Littlestone Links Golf Club. Reflecting its status, it was at the time comfortably the largest hotel on this part of the coast. Visitors would be met by taxi at New Romney Station and driven the very short distance to the Grand. Here they would be joined in the bar by those prominent members of society who had bought their own properties in the village.

By the 1920's it was flourishing and an advert from the period shows that the hotel offered a drawing room overlooking the foreshore, a billiard room and a garage and inspection pit, allied to the opportunity to hire a car by the hour, day or week. At this time it also boasted the rather quaint telephone number of New Romney 7.

Its popularity was short-lived, however. Whilst visitors still flocked to the golf links, the Grand Hotel was soon eclipsed by the neighbouring Dormy House Hotel. After surviving a serious fire in 1936, it twice suffered serious damage during the war when trading as Pope's Hotel;[8] in October 1942 it was struck by a bomb (photographs show a neat hole through the side of the building) and then in August 1944 a doodlebug (a V1 flying bomb) fell to ground on the beach just in front of the building, with the resultant explosion smashing the hotel roof.

---

8. The name "Pope's Hotel" refelected a change of ownership, Arthur Pope being a co-owner.

The Grand Hotel in the 1930s (top left); WWII bomb damage to Pope's (top right); under demolition in 1973 (bottom left: photo copyright John Baker and licensed for reuse under a Creative Commons Licence); and flats (Grand Court) standing on the site in 2014 (bottom right)

Fortunes didn't improve and, despite a further name change – to The Ferry – it never recaptured its glory days. It was demolished in 1973.

Grasshopper Hotel (Mary Ross Grasshopper Hotel), 3 Littlestone Road, New Romney, TN28 8LN

The property at 3 Littlestone Road has had a number of incarnations. It seems that it first had a licence in the 1970s, when it enjoyed some success as the Grasshopper Hotel, trading on its proximity to the RH&DR station. It was still operating as such up until the end of the 1980s (and possibly into the 1990s), but by 2000 it was a nightclub, under the guise of The Avenue Club. Its major selling point has been a basement that can accommodate up to 200 guests, and since then its activities – whilst encompassing various forms of dancing and karaoke –

The Littlestone Hotel (formerly the Grasshopper Hotel)

have been quite heavily regulated by the licensing authorities (and often only operating from Thursday to Sunday). It currently trades as the Littlestone Hotel, with self-catering facilities.

Romney Bay House, Coast Road, Littlestone, TN28 8QY

This pleasing 1920s building is situated along the track (it can't really be termed a road for much of its length) between Littlestone and St Mary's Bay. Overlooking the sea and backing onto the Littlestone Golf Club, it has an enviable location. It was designed at the time that Littlestone was starting to develop by no less an architect than Sir Clough Williams-Ellis.[9] Furthermore, it was commissioned by Hollywood starlet (and later celebrity gossip columnist) Hedda Hopper. Her liking for bright colours was not widely shared by her neighbours, who

Romney Bay House

---

9. Renowned for creating the Italianate village of Portmeirion in North Wales.

christened it "the mustard pot"! Over the years it has seen service in a number of different guises, but mostly as a hotel. Although currently trading as a hotel and restaurant, it serves alcohol only to its guests; but in the 1970s through to the 1990s it had a popular bar open to non-residents.

Lydd-on-sea

Lydd-on-sea could be seen as Greatstone's younger sister, as it comprises mainly seaside bungalow development along the coast road to Dungeness. The main difference between the two communities is that nearly all building work in Lydd-on-sea was undertaken after WWII. But as with Greatstone, Lydd-on-sea was one of the only two beneficiaries of the re-routing of the railway in 1937. Its station was also very poorly used and, like its counterpart, closed in 1967.

The name reflects that the parish of Lydd – once itself coastal – is now several miles inland. It has had only the one pub to its name, although some guides have also placed the Ship (Lade) within the boundaries of Lydd-on-sea.

The Pilot Inn, Battery Road, Lydd-on-sea, TN29 9NJ

There is much confusion over the history of this pub, which almost certainly started life in Dungeness. But it has moved northward over the years and now sits just inside the Lydd-on-sea boundary. There is also uncertainty over just when the Pilot name was adopted, and by what names it may have formerly been known.[10]

The Pilot has its roots in a rather dark episode in local history. There was already a crude building on the beach near to the present site when, at some time in the 17th century, a three-masted frigate/schooner by the name of the *Alfresia* was lured onto the beach, its crew murdered and its cargo of gold, wine and spirits looted. There is even debate over exactly when this occurred, although the widely accepted date is 1633. Other contenders include 1624 and 1644, but it is possible that the former is the date of establishment of the original inn. Whatever the date, the hold of the ill-fated *Alfresia* was used to augment the structure of the existing building and, for many years, formed the ceiling of what subsequently became the saloon bar. It has been claimed that part of this ship stayed *in situ* right up until the late 1950s. This is most unlikely, because of the evidence of the Pilot "migrating" a short distance during its various incarnations, and also because significant redevelopment took place in 1823. It is further claimed that the Pilot is haunted by a passenger from the *Alfresia*: a grey lady, who clearly has little self-respect as she inhabits what is now the toilet area.

Wrecking was not the only shady activity to keep the locals busy; there was much smuggling centred on the inn – which incorporated sliding hatches from which the smugglers could signal to boats at sea. There are reports of fierce encounters taking place here between

---

10. See also Dungeness entries for the Dover Hoveller and Jolly Sailor.

The Pilot in 1910 (top) was similar in appearance to the Hope & Anchor at Dungeness; whilst its 1957 incarnation (above) was also unoriginal, being almost indistinguishable from the nearby Britannia

Court Blockade officers and smugglers, with some of the former being captured and lashed to tubs before being sent to their deaths at sea; and of revenue officers being shot and buried nearby on the Lydd road.

The Tart fishing family[11] ran the Pilot for very many years, and records show that, in 1910, it was a fully licensed restaurant/inn of timber construction, with three sitting rooms, four bedrooms and a cellar.

Not many pubs can claim to have their own railway station, but this was the case with the Pilot for a number of years. When the RH&DR opened its Dungeness extension, it initially terminated here and the Pilot railway station opened on 24 May 1928. On full completion of the line – to the lighthouse – in August 1928, the station was retained, but re-classified as a halt. The station building remained unaltered until demolition in 1967, but was replaced with a breeze block shelter the following year. It was a popular stop with locals, who took advantage of the railway's weekly discounted shopper specials to New Romney and Hythe, and with

---

11. See also entry for the Hope & Anchor, Dungeness.

The much more modern Pilot building, in 2012

those who found it more convenient and pleasant to travel by a steam-hauled train to enjoy their pint at the pub. It continued to serve as a request stop on the line until 1977, although special trains continued to stop by arrangement and the Pilot Halt remained listed in the RH&DR timetable up until 1993.

During WWII the pub was taken over by the army, as were all properties in the area, and suffered from some none too gentle treatment. But things could have been worse: in November 1943, a British aircraft returning from a mission dropped nine incendiary bombs on the beach, unaware that the Pilot was almost directly underneath. Despite some damage to its windows, however, the structure survived intact. The Pilot also featured in the incredibly successful fund-raising initiative *Salute the Soldier Week* in May/June 1943, hosting a mobile cinema van in its car park.

By 1957, the timber building – exposed to the elements as it was – was deemed to be no longer repairable and it was replaced by a new modern structure. This did not share the same footprint as the previous building, moving to the eastern side of the RH&DR line. At this time, the owners rather imaginatively marketed the pub under the banner: Operation **P**atrons **L**ook **U**p **T**he **O**ld Pilot Inn![12] At this time, it was still possible to hire boats from here; and outside the pub was an upturned boat, which served as a herring hang for smoking bloaters.

Another significant upgrade was completed in 2012. The position of the Pilot Inn affords its customers excellent views of shipping in the Channel, and seating and tables have been sited to take full advantage of this. It is not surprising that the pub has, over the years, also taken advantage of the availability of locally caught fresh fish and, accordingly, gained a strong reputation for its fish and chip meals. These factors combine to ensure that the Pilot continues to enjoy a very healthy trade. The Pilot also remains one of the very few pubs in the country where ring-the-bull can still be played, continuing a tradition that stretches back nearly a hundred years.

---

12. This references the wartime PLUTO (Pipeline under the Ocean) project; see also the Jolly Fisherman at Greatstone.

The lighthouse depicted in the background of the Pilot's former inn sign was a faithful representation of the fourth lighthouse constructed in 1901. When in use, it was painted in this likeness (the current all-black colour scheme of the old light is to avoid confusion with its successor, constructed in 1961). This sign now hangs inside the pub

The Pilot name, of course, derives from one of the oldest maritime professions – the practice of an experienced local mariner boarding ships to guide them through dangerous or congested waters. The channel waters around here are deep and treacherous and, prior to the introduction of electronic shipping aids, such pilots were mandatory for shipping of any significant size. The pub sign displayed up until 2014 was a pleasing representation, with the Dungeness lighthouse clearly shown in the background.

St Mary's Bay

St Mary's Bay owes its existence largely to the holiday trade and until 1935 was known as Jesson. In the 1940s it was a tiny hamlet, which had few amenities and no pub of any description. During the war it had its own air strip, one of the four Advanced Landing Grounds (ALGs) on Romney Marsh. The first and only *bona fide* pub was established in the 1950s and survives to this day. The 'Bay' has, however, had a number of other clubs and licensed establishments, the most prominent of which were the **Pirates Spring Country Club** and the **Nightrider Club**. Neither still operates. The former was located on Coast Drive, not far from the beach, and was originally a venue for mentally handicapped children (operated by the forerunner of Mencap). This operation closed in the 1980s and the building subsequently became a hotel and country club. The Nightrider Club, where bat-and-trap was played, was sited next to Jenner's coal yard, between the A259 and New Sewer. It was demolished in the 1990s and the site, along with the coal yard itself, is now occupied by houses. Both clubs served non-members, although these may have been unofficial arrangements.

St Mary's Bay remains defined by its holiday trade and has its own station (now a request stop) on the RH&DR, which skirts the village to the north.

Bahia Bar, Dymchurch Road, St Mary's Bay

The 1920s' single-storey Sands Hotel was built on what was then known as "The Outlands", which originally belonged to Jesson Farm. This is on the seafront opposite the A259/Jefferstone Lane junction and, until this time, would often be under water when the sea seeped through the wall (it was only enhancements to the sea wall that enabled construction of the hotel). The hotel comprised three surplus army huts, and one of these contained a bar. Ironically, during WWII, it was commandeered by the army and during this time was struck by a bomb, which killed numerous servicemen and caused severe damage. The hotel did re-open, but with only limited success before it was demolished in 1970. The Sands Holiday Motel emerged phoenix-like from the ashes the following year, and the Bahia Bar was constructed in the winter of 1975/6 as part of the same complex. The exotic name (shared with that of a Brazilian state) is a loose translation of the Portuguese word for "bay".

1970s' advert for the Bahia Bar

The Bahia sought to emulate the continental bars that were becoming so popular with package-holiday tourists at this time, and this featured heavily in the motel's advertising. It was, however, out of keeping with the Kent coastal atmosphere and, when badly damaged in the 1987 storm, was closed. Temporary repairs were effected, but, after further storm damage inflicted two years later, the building was demolished in 1990.

The site of the former Sands Holiday Motel and Bahia bar – still undeveloped in 2013

Bailiff's Sargeant, Jefferstone Lane, St Mary's Bay, TN29 0SA

Following the aforementioned post-war expansion of St Mary's Bay, Mackeson's identified a gap in the market and sought to establish a community pub, but were hampered by the economic hardship that was one of the many legacies of WWII. In particular, there was a chronic shortage of building materials, which meant that a new build was unviable. Mackeson's accordingly looked to a ready-built solution and identified the 1930-built Jesson Stores and off-licence in Jefferstone Lane for their purposes. They purchased the freehold and completed the conversion in February 1951. The former shopkeeper was engaged as landlord, which illustrates just how employment practices have changed over the years.

Another obstacle at this time was the draconian planning restrictions that applied to building conversions, and Mackeson's were not granted the necessary authority to make all the changes they wished. A number of compromises had to be made and, as a result, the side entrance became the off-sales department and the former garage encompassed two unlikely – and frankly unhygienic – bedfellows: the lavatories and beer store! For reasons lost in the mists of time, for many years locals referred to it as "The Rat and Cat".

The Bailiff's Sergeant, pictured shortly after opening (top – photo: David Harper) and in 2013

55

The proper name of the pub reflects the ancient and important Marsh position of the *Bailiff of the Lord's Jurats and Commonalty of Romney Marsh*, and the then incumbent (Major Teichmann-Derville) and his sergeant (in full office uniform) performed the opening ceremony. The following year, with building restrictions now eased, Mackeson's acquired the adjacent May Cottage and the pub was rebuilt to incorporate it, leaving the exterior of the building much as it is today. Whitbread leased the pub to Shepherd Neame in 1992, who subsequently purchased the freehold in 1996. Those who care about the English language will be disappointed that the Bailiff's apostrophe has been dropped somewhere along the way!

3

Marsh Villages

There are many qualities that make Romney Marsh special, and not least are the contrasts to be found. Whilst the coastal resorts can be crowded in the summer and moody and windswept in the winter, the inland villages offer peace and tranquillity. On a sunny summer's day on the Marsh, you can find yourself seemingly transported miles from the stresses of everyday life, surrounded by farmland, meadows and birdsong, underneath the area's famed "big skies". Throw in one of the Marsh's outstandingly beautiful churches and a pint in a comfortable hostelry and you have the quintessential English village scenario.

Elsewhere in this book, the loss of Newchurch's only pub and the attendant impact upon the appeal of the village have been lamented. But, objectively, it is probably more pertinent to record that most of the remaining villages – despite very small populations – still support at least one pub, which is not only surviving but, in many cases, thriving.

Appledore

Once a busy shipbuilding town – a port on a branch of the estuary of the River Rother – the small village of Appledore has an interesting history stretching back to Roman times. It has even been involved in issues of national importance, as the Danes made it their base for an invasion of England in 892 AD. Villagers also took part in the 1381 Peasants' Revolt led by Wat Tyler, and in Jack Cade's rebellion against Henry VI in 1450.

The village straddles the Marsh, with the bulk of its properties being to the north of the Royal Military Canal, whilst the station is fully a mile away by road from the community it purports to serve. This was not an uncommon scenario at a time when railways tended to follow the long, straight principles embodied by the Romans and the convenience of residents was not a major consideration.

One of the first recorded pubs in the village was the Queen's Arms, although there may well have been another pub prior to this as the 16th century building known as Bennett's[1] was listed as The Bell when purchased by Mr Bennett in 1658. Its earlier name firmly suggests an alcoholic connection, but no further details can be found. Records do show that there were two pubs in the village in 1847, with a further beer shop (off licence) owned by Elizabeth

---

1. Post code TN26 2AE; OS reference TQ955297.

Packham. 50 years on from then the number of pubs had doubled, with the Victoria and Railway Inn having joined the Red Lion and Swan. Sadly, however, only one is still open for business, although even that has undergone a change of name.

Queen's Arms, 1/2 Court Lodge Road, Appledore, TN26 2DD

On the corner of Court Lodge Road and the Street, this was a mediaeval house first referred to as the Queen's Arms in 1706, although it would most probably have served as a tavern prior to this. The name is attributed to an incident when Queen Anne visited Appledore by river barge and was allegedly given a glass of water drawn from the garden well here. Prior to this incident, the property had – for obvious reasons – been known as Well House. Up until the construction of the Royal Military Canal (i.e. prior to the late 18th century), the garden of the Queen's Arms adjoined that of Vine House, although The Street now separates the two. In the 19th century the property, no longer serving as a pub, was owned by historian Dr William Cock, who extended it to the west. After his death (in 1941) it was divided into two separate dwellings.

Railway Hotel, Station Road, Appledore, TN26 2DF

The LB&SCR opened its Hastings to Ashford line in 1851 and the Railway Hotel was constructed soon after. This was the only one of three hotels built on the Marsh to serve the various railway branches to have retained its original name by the end of the 20th century. Disappointingly, in 2013 it became the second to close its doors.

*The house that was once the
Queen's Arms*

Left: The Railway Hotel © Copyright Simon Carey and licensed for reuse under a Creative Commons Licence. Right: The Railway's accommodation block, sealed off in 2013 and now demolished. Note the railway signal installed in the garden, denoting whether the pub was open for business

Notwithstanding, it had bucked the trend for a number of years, in spite of its remote location. Unusually having added extensive motel accommodation behind the main building, it built up an enviable reputation in the 1980s and 1990s. It also hosted a thriving folk club and marketed a bike hire business, which appealed not only to holidaymakers, but also to inhabitants of Hastings and Ashford, who would combine a relaxing train journey across the Marsh with some gentle exercise on the tranquil Marsh lanes, which are renowned for good cycling. Others would take the same rail journey, but with a satisfying pub lunch as their only goal.

The harsh realities of the current economy and its location meant that the Railway's future was limited. Not even the proposed upgrade of the railway line could save it (the likelihood being that high-speed services between Hastings and Ashford will only stop at Rye). The hotel was converted into a private dwelling in 2014, and the accommodation block demolished at the same time to make way for housing.

Black Lion (Red Lion), 15 The Street, Appledore, TN26 2BU

Situated at the southern end of the village, just before you cross the Royal Military Canal, is an attractive Georgian brick house with a fine portico and with the Norman parish church behind it – the Black Lion.

For most of its life this building (as well as its predecessor) was known as the Red Lion. Once a general store with stables attached, it initially occupied a site opposite the current pub, which later became the village forge. It subsequently (on its new site) became a stopping point for the Jubilee coach, which ran between Tenterden and Appledore Station. At this time it was a jettied, timber-framed building to which was later added weatherboarding. In 1810 it is recorded that it was being used to host auction sales and, by 1852, was part of the estate

The Black Lion in 2013

owned by Rye's Albion Brewery. By the 1920s it was in the hands of Style and Winch, but by this time it was in a poor state of repair. It was thus pulled down in December 1932 and replaced by the current imposing brick building of traditional country design (now attractively clad in ivy).

Fulfilling an important village need, the postman and others would leave letters and packages at the Red Lion for collection and, until the imposition of the hunting ban, the Ashford Hunt would meet here once or twice every winter. At one time, the Romney Marsh Harriers (foxhounds) would also meet here on a regular basis. In the 1980s, it created quite a reputation for cuisine that was out of the ordinary, an example of which was the rather intriguing halibut with banana and mango chutney sauce! After a short closure and change of ownership in 1997, it then became the Black Lion in 2003.

Whilst some sources have linked the new name to the heraldic sign of Queen Phillipa of Hainault (wife of Edward III), the reasons for the change were not rooted in history. The new landlord had previously run the Black Horse at Monks Horton and before that another pub whose name had incorporated the same colour. The change was not widely popular, but the new owner quickly forged good links and, by way of compromise, it is known to all in the locality as "The Lion". It is used as a meeting place for local campanologists (the Appledore Ringers).

Swan Hotel, 27 The Street, Appledore, TN26 2BU

The original Swan was a fine building constructed in about 1740, becoming an alehouse very shortly after. Its early history shows it owned by two different Lydd brewers – Thomas

Heisell and Alfred White. It appears in *Pigot's Directory* of 1828–29 and served as a coaching inn before being registered as a hotel in 1873.

SWAN HOTEL
Appledore

The premises were rebuilt in 1910, although some of the original fabric (including most of the stables) was retained. Significant extension was undertaken in 1926, with the addition of a public room, and in 1927 the stables were converted to garages. For much of its later life it was a Whitbread/Fremlins house, and was the foremost of Appledore's inns. At various times it offered five or six bedrooms, sleeping up to 15 guests. This pub was a popular base through the 1980s with contract sheep shearers from New Zealand, whose maxim was to work hard and play hard. In those less enlightened times, drink driving rules were often ignored and many a shearer's car would be found upturned in ditches on the nearby lanes, often as the result of a trip back from the Woolpack at Brookland. During the latter part of the 20th century there was a high turnover of landlords, one of whom (during the 1990s) was very popular despite his intimidating appearance. Sporting a shaved head and Fu Manchu moustache, for 38 years he was better known as the Mighty Mongol, a regular on the professional wrestling circuit.

The Swan featured in the third series of *Whitbread inn signs* in 1951. Although some older guide books referred to the *White Swan* (presumably based on the sign), there is no evidence that this was ever its formal name. One of that select band of Marsh pubs where it was possible to play ring-the-bull, the Swan closed sometime after September 2006, and is now private accommodation (fittingly named, with a nod to local history, *Cygnet Cottage*).

The Swan in its heyday (late 1940s – photo David Harper); and Cygnet Cottage in 2014

Victoria Inn (Arms), Appledore Heath

The Victoria (at the northern end of the village, close to Heathside) was not listed in the village directory of 1847, so its appearance in 1897 listings suggests that it opened at some time in the intervening period – but before 1864, as a newspaper report of that year recorded the landlord injuring himself in a shooting accident. This same report refers to the pub as the Victoria Arms. Part of Finn's estate, it was listed as a freehold beerhouse when auctioned in 1921. Thereafter, it earned a reputation as a slightly rough pub, popular with both soldiers and local youths – who were not too closely questioned about their age. Still listed in directories of 1982, it closed soon after and was demolished to make way for private housing in the mid-1990s. At the time of writing, its last landlady – Hilda Pratt – still lives in the village.

Bonnington

If the case for including Appledore amongst the Romney Marsh villages may be open to debate, that for Bonnington is, at first sight, even more tenuous. This is a sprawling settlement, based mainly on the hills to the north of the Royal Military Canal; but the only pub that has ever graced it is some two and a half miles from the village centre – and very much within the Marsh boundaries. Never any larger than today (it has less than 100 residents), Bonnington had strong links to smuggling and at one time boasted its own school and church, as well as the public house. The parish church – dedicated to St Rumbold – is all that remains of this triumvirate today.

Royal Oak, The Street, Bonnington, TN25 7BP

Even by the area's own standards, the Royal Oak was remote. It is mentioned by GM Rainbird in his rather charming 1948 book *The Inns of Kent*. The author was clearly given a remit that comprised a list of pubs to review but reports that he twice drove within a short distance of the Royal Oak without actually finding it! He goes on to say: "that the Royal Oak exists would seem to be confirmed in that sundry barrels of good ale are consigned to it weekly by the brewers at Hythe"!

The property is no easier to locate today. Nearer to Newchurch than the bulk of Bonnington, it stands on crossroads between Hurst Farm and Bellfield Farm and is probably best sought by its grid reference: TR0711932874 (co-ordinates 607119, 132874). Records date the building to 1748, when it was a private house, and it was not until 1828–29 that it was first listed as a pub (within *Pigot's National & Commercial Directory*). The wheel has turned full circle, with conversion back to a private dwelling, after it ceased trading in 1971. It is now known as the Old Oak.

It is something of a mystery how pubs as remote as this can have survived for any length of time, and there was very little winter trade. David Harper has identified that only 27 barrels

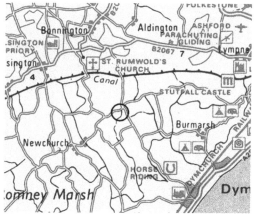

The location of the Bonnington Oak (circled) (© Philip's; Reproduced by permission of Ordnance Survey on behalf of HMSO. © Crown copyright 100043101. All rights reserved.)

were sold in 1951, an incredibly low volume. Whilst this figure would – must – have been higher in previous years, it is inevitable, therefore, that some landlords looked to supplement their income with less legitimate activities. The Bonnington Oak (as it was more commonly known) was very popular with the smuggling fraternity, and members of the infamous Ransley family were frequent patrons. Whilst the Ransleys were more commonly associated with the Walnut Tree at Aldington, they would think nothing of making the three mile trip through the winding lanes to the Royal Oak and tales are told of them playing darts by the light of a paraffin lamp. They were also in the habit of ordering and receiving their beer – literally – by the bucketload! In the 1820s the landlord was listed as a Mr Huckstead and there is much evidence to link the Huckstead family with the free trade – notwithstanding that most of this is circumstantial. What can more definitely be confirmed is that, following a major smuggling "run" at Hythe in March 1826, a number of smugglers were injured in a skirmish with blockade men and the gang repaired to the Royal Oak, where the wounded were patched up and refreshment obtained. Interviewed by customs officers, Huckstead later failed to recall seeing any of them on the night in question!

The Royal Oak is also credited as being one of the Mackeson's houses where the John Jones Coursing Club would meet on Monday nights (see Chapter 1). It was a gem of its time and – endearingly – only had electricity laid on in 1968, just three years before its demise.

The Royal Oak in the 1950s (left; photo: David Harper) and back in private use in 2014

Botolph's Bridge

Despite its West Hythe postal code, Botolph's Bridge is a discrete, tiny settlement to the north of Dymchurch and east of Burmarsh. The area has been known by many names (each reflecting its status as a crossing point), including Boter's, Butter's and Butler's Bridge. In 1801 it was described as Buttolph's Bridge; by 1821 it had become Bitolph's Bridge; and by 1847, Buttolphus Bridge. But all these are just minor variations on the current name. Just why a hamlet and pub on Romney Marsh should be dedicated to a seventh-century Saxon abbot with strong links to Lincolnshire is open to conjecture. But the most likely explanation is that displaced Lincolnshire farmers who found the marsh geology to their liking brought some of their culture with them.

A number of official footpath and cycling routes pass through the village and provide an excellent introduction to the Marsh. Particularly on a misty autumnal day, the solitude of Botolph's Bridge can be the complete antidote to stressful town life and offers an insight into how smuggling could have once taken such a hold on the community.

Botolph's Bridge Inn, Botolph's Bridge Road, West Hythe, Hythe, CT21 4NL

This is one of a number of hostelries whose remoteness means that it can quite justifiably lay claim to truly represent the mood and spirit of the Marsh. Records show the existence of a pub on the current site (at the junction of Botolph's Bridge, West Hythe and Burmarsh Roads and alongside a branch of the Royal Military Canal) in 1726, and that it was one of the John Friend houses acquired by Mackeson's in 1801.

The Botolph's Bridge pictured in 1980. Pubmaster changed the inn sign in 1990; this move was not well received by the public so, to their credit, they agreed to revert to the original design. However the previous sign had been destroyed and a new one had to be produced using a laser image of the 1951 collector's miniature (above right)

The pub's location has resulted in it often leading a marginal existence. Accordingly, it has worked hard to integrate with the local community and has been the home for such diverse organisations as motor cycling clubs and the East Kent Morris Dancers. Bat-and-trap was once a staple activity, and the pub has also fielded its own cricket team. Up until the late 20th century, ring-the-bull could be played and, before the opening of the RAF museum at Brenzett, the pub sported RAF memorabilia (which have now been donated to the museum). More recently it has hosted a petanque team. The original building became tired and dilapidated and was rebuilt before WWII, re-opening in 1937. In its current form the building itself is pretty unremarkable. The pub now survives on its restaurant trade.

The intriguing inn sign depicts not an episode from the Doctor Syn novels (as erroneously stated in some sources) but the story of St Botolph. Legend has it that, in a bid to protect it from desecration by the marauding Danes, the body of St Botolph was moved from its resting place. This took place on a dark, cloudy night, and the monks charged with the task were struggling to cross a body of water when, suddenly, a shaft of light appeared to guide them.

Brenzett

Ten miles due south of Ashford and six miles north east of Rye, with a population of 500, the village of Brenzett was immortalised in verse by Rudyard Kipling: "Oh Romney Level and Brenzett reeds . . . I reckon you know what my heart needs . . .". During WWII, Brenzett was one of the locations on the Marsh to host an Advanced Landing Ground and the area's aviation history is recalled in the excellent Brenzett Aeronautical Museum. Further back in time, in 1381, the village was the rallying point for supporters of Wat Tyler's peasants' revolt. Unfortunately, the fate of Brenzett mirrors that of many small villages, with the recent closure of village shops and its one pub. The hub of the village is accordingly now the local primary school, but that was also threatened with closure only recently. Although earning a reprieve, its future is very much dependent on the birth rate.

Fleur-de-Lys, Rhee Wall Road, Brenzett, TN29 9UG

There is conflicting information about the origins of this building, although it was certainly in existence in 1694/95, and may date back even further. Sited at the western end of the village on the crossroads of the B2080 New Romney to Tenterden and the then main Ashford Road, this detached three-storey timber-framed building was originally a farmhouse. It served a number of functions before assuming the name of the Fleur-de-Lys in 1820. When open, it had the distinction of being one of the few Marsh pubs with a cellar.

Used by the land army in WWII, the pub reopened after the cessation of hostilities and traded successfully for many years. Its commercial success was largely down to its location, although, ironically, this resulted in an increase in traffic noise levels that was not appreciated by its customers. As a result, the corner door (see photographs) was blocked up in an attempt

The Fleur de Lys c. 1910 (left) and in sadder circumstances in 2013

to reduce noise inside the pub. What is also of interest in the old pictures is how the level of the road has risen over the past 100 years or so. Successive levels of resurfacing have had the effect of significantly reducing the gap between the bottom of the pub doors and the road.

More than just a pub, though, the Fleur de Lys also offered accommodation.[2] It closed around 2009 and the accommodation area was converted to office training rooms. Now boarded up, it is sadly unlikely to re-open in its former capacity.

Brookland

Brookland was also featured by Kipling within *Puck of Pooks Hill*, where one of the characters, describing the uniqueness of Romney Marsh, alludes to "steeples settin' beside churches". This is a reference to the church of St Augustine, where the steeple sits on the ground next to the church. There are a number of explanations as to how this strange situation came about. You may choose to believe that the steeple jumped off in surprise when a bride turned up to be married without being pregnant; or that the architect didn't have a sufficiently large piece of paper and drew the steeple by the side – with the builder constructing it as drawn. Or you may take the less romantic but more pragmatic view that the marsh geology was not strong enough to support the full structure.

In addition to a church separated from its bell tower, the village is also famous as the site of the infamous Battle of Brookland, waged between local smugglers and the authorities in 1821. This was notable for the high level of casualties: four smugglers were left dead and 16 wounded; against one dead and eight wounded amongst the Blockade men who had pursued the smugglers from Camber.

At the southern end of the village can be found a go-kart track. This marks part of the site of a large WWII army camp. After the camp closed, the Nissan huts and other buildings

---

2. In 1987, it was still advertising four rooms, accommodating up to 12 guests.

St Augustine's Church, Brookland, 2012 – seen from the Royal Oak

were maintained as the rather unlikely setting for a replica Filipino village, which doubled as a craft centre. This survived for many years, and hosted an annual Filipino re-union and celebration, which drew visitors from all over the globe.

Realignment of the A259 road at the end of the 1980s perversely meant that parts of the village became bypassed and reverted to how they would have looked prior to the invention of the internal combustion engine. However, it did have the less desirable impact of cutting the village in two.

Alliance Inn, 10 Rye Road, Brookland, TN29 9RA

The Alliance was once a common pub name, commemorating the agreement with Scotland in the reign of Queen Anne. Although a number of pubs marked this event, there were very few so named in the south east of England.

At one time, this was the most prominent of Brookland's inns. Although slightly smaller than the Royal Oak, its prime location on the New Romney to Rye road meant that it was well situated to attract the passing trade. It formed part of the "stable" of Edwin Finn's pubs and boasted three bars, coach house and stabling for three horses.

Sold on to Style & Winch in 1921, the Alliance suffered minor bomb damage (its first floor windows being blown out) in early 1944, but its death blow was the aforementioned re-

The Alliance in its heyday (1930s, left) and in private use (2013)

routing of the main road. Locals still recall with amusement that the captain of the Brookland cricket team would offer £5 for any batsman who could hit the roof of the Alliance.[3] The pub struggled throughout the late 1970s and 1980s and closed as a pub in 1984 or 1985, although for a short time re-opening as a restaurant and tea rooms. It is now a family home; although less easy to spot from the main road because of the latter's realignment; a slight detour reveals that it remains very recognisable (although the porch and one of its chimneys have since been removed).

Although no longer a pub, a small part of the Alliance lived on for many years. Strangely, its curtains were removed and transferred to the nearby Woolpack, where they remained until 2015.

Royal Oak (Yew and Ewe), High Street, Brookland, TN29 9QR

This Grade II listed building houses another charismatic Marsh pub that has a number of claims to fame, one of which is by virtue of its location next to the unique Brookland church. The largest of Brookland's inns, it has not, however, been without its darker side over the years.

The proximity of the pub and church is no co-incidence: the building was originally (in the 1570s) constructed as a dwelling for the parish clerk and sexton. It was not until 1736 that a liquor licence was granted, although the authorities showed unusual sensitivity by adding the caveat that ale was "not to be tippled during divine service".

Fighting at the aforementioned Battle of Brookland centred around the Royal Oak, and bodies were laid out and the injured treated inside the pub. If you are easily offended by the thought of blood and gore, the Royal Oak probably wouldn't have been the pub for you in the 19th and early 20th centuries either, as a slaughterhouse was established just behind the premises. This is quite prominent in early photographs of the pub, as is the distinctive garage (this was subsequently absorbed into the pub; the former garage door becoming a bar entrance).

---

3. The cricket field was then much closer than the current facility, and was destroyed to facilitate the A259 road realignment.

The Royal Oak between the wars (top) and in 2013 (bottom)

It is no surprise that a pub in the heart of a village like Brookland would be the hub of the community and this was the case, certainly through much of the 19th and 20th centuries. Amongst other sporting and social games, cricket was a particular passion and, throughout the 1950s, the then landlord Mr Lambert and his wife were in the habit of throwing lavish Christmas parties attended by upwards of 50 of the local children.

There have been internal alterations and some cosmetic changes to the outside of the building, but pictures of the pub from the 1920s show that (with the exception of the garage) little has significantly altered over the last 100 years. As with many village pubs, the Royal Oak suffered economic hardship at the turn of the millennium and closed for a time. It was subsequently purchased by two couples and re-opened in October 2004, but under the name of the Yew and Ewe. For those who do not believe that it is bad luck to change the name of a pub, this provides a salutary lesson: in July 2005 – in a case that received national news coverage – one of the joint owners bludgeoned his wife as she slept. She may well have died but for the intervention of the couple's ten-year-old daughter. At the subsequent trial it was claimed that the husband had plotted to murder her and pretend that she had committed suicide by walking into the sea at Dungeness (he had driven her car and clothes to the beach and jogged back to the pub).[4]

In April 2006 the pub was sold to Enterprise Inns and the name reverted to the Royal Oak (and rightly so!). The same year, Prince Edward's brother-in-law, David Rhys-Jones, became licensee. This resulted in a blaze of publicity, in which it was claimed that Prince Edward himself had been a regular visitor to the pub, retiring there following shooting parties at Sissinghurst. It is likely that these claims were – at best – highly exaggerated, but most of the national newspaper reviews were highly favourable. By November 2012, however, these were tailing off and the Royal Oak closed again, with the same newspapers reporting that Rhys-Jones had incurred debts in excess of £100k. It reopened under new ownership and management in July 2013.

Woolpack, A259, Brookland, TN29 9TJ

There was a building on this site from 1410, when the sea lapped against its walls, and it served as a beacon keeper's house. Some of the 15th century construction (beams and wattle-and-daub) remains within the current fabric of the Woolpack.

The Woolpack is a bona fide smuggler's pub, once used by the infamous Aldington Gang, and with plenty of evidence to support its links to the free trade. In 1890 the Bagnall family were listed as keepers and, although smuggling had peaked by this time, their ancestors were almost certainly key players in local activities. There are still traces of a secret passage once used to evade capture by excise officers and, if you sit at the long table in the main bar, the strange item that you will see wedged on the ceiling between the beams above your head is a "spinning jenny". There is more than one theory as to its purpose, but the most popular is that it is a device used to distribute the spoils of a successful smuggling "run". The table at which you are sitting bears testimony to a different form of gambling: it incorporates a shove-penny board, the larger than usual spaces denoting that it was played with the "cartwheel" pennies popular in Georgian times. Other items of genuine historic interest to be found adorning this two-room hostelry include an ancient Flanders tapestry and a mediaeval lock that was in use up until 1972.

This is a classic country pub, a whitewashed building with an inglenook fireplace and hop bines adorning old beams – some of which are claimed to have come from local shipwrecks. It was deemed to be an excellent setting for scenes within the 1947 film *The Loves of Joanna Godden*, a film that is recommended viewing for anyone with an interest in the Romney Marsh. The producers of this film financed the installation of hitching posts, which remained in place until relatively recently.

---

4.   He was cleared of attempted murder, however, and his plea of guilty to grievous bodily harm accepted.

The Woolpack was a regular Boxing Day venue for the local hunt (left, 1930s). The fabric of the pub has changed little over the years (right, 1988)

The pub was for many years the traditional Boxing Day rendezvous for the Romney Marsh Hunt. Although the ban on fox hunting saw a temporary end to this tradition, in recent years the occasional drag hunt has started from here. The Woolpack also remains a favourite haunt of anglers fishing the nearby White Kemp sewer. Its resident ghost – a flute player – appears to have shied away from the limelight in recent years.

Burmarsh

This small village, some four miles to the south west of Hythe and next to the Royal Military Canal, is one of the earliest settlements on Romney Marsh, dating from the 12th century. The land once belonged to the burghers (citizens) of Canterbury, from which the village name derives.

Shepherd & Crook, Shear Way, Burmarsh, TN29 0JJ

Another Romney Marsh gem, the Shepherd and Crook is another genuinely old (and listed) building. Just how old, however, is open to conjecture. Sources record a building here in the 16th century, although much of the current structure dates from around 1750. However, it has also been claimed that, in the 15th century, the King's Hospitallers provided food, drink and shelter for weary travellers and knights and monks on pilgrimages to Canterbury from here; and also that parts of the building are even of the same stone as the adjacent 12th century church.

What is more verifiable is that the Shepherd & Crook did not formally become a pub until 1801 and has a history of ownership by established Marsh families, being operated in the mid-

The Shepherd & Crook, c. 1930s (top). It remains instantly recognisable in this 1980 photograph (above), although – since then – the construction of a housing estate has altered the surroundings somewhat. An annexe was also added in 2010

1860s by the Piddocks (who also owned the Botolphs Bridge Inn) and later that century by the Hucksteps (additionally licensees of the Royal Oak at Bonnington).

Burmarsh and the Shepherd & Crook have for centuries been involved with sheep farming and, inevitably, smuggling (and also feature in the *Doctor Syn* novels). In the late 19th century, the pub was arguably one of the four local venues for the John Jones Coursing Club. At the turn of the 20th century, the pub became the home for Sunday services when the church was being renovated. During WWII, soldiers were billeted both here and at the nearby vicarage. A story is told that the colonel made himself deeply unpopular by dint of commandeering the only decent bed and that his subordinates responded by capturing a lamb and putting it in the bed with him! However, for a long time the pub was noted for being a very quiet one, right up until 1957 when it was sold by Whitbread and became a free house. The upstairs room was then turned into a dance hall and the place flourished.

The pub, a grade II listed building, suffered significant damage in the great storm of 1987, with the loss of numerous windows and a chimney toppling and crashing through the roof. Soon fully restored, the pub offers a lovely glimpse of village life in the summer via its sheltered garden, and has a welcoming open fire in winter months.

The Shepherd & Crook has for long displayed items of local history as well as antiques, and these have included a pair of Queen Victoria's stockings.

Ivychurch

Whilst the parish of Ivychurch is huge, the village itself is not and numbers only around a hundred or so inhabitants. Nonetheless, it will not be a great surprise to learn that it boasts a sizeable pub and an enormous church. The village lies just to the north west of Old Romney and its name does simply translate as "ivy-covered church".

The Bell Inn, Ashford Road, Ivychurch TN29 0AL

The Bell Inn was built in 1545, on the site of a much older mediaeval building – which may well also have been a hostelry. The name is very much in accordance with the custom of the time: the adjacent church of St George had just the one bell.[5] The beer garden backs onto the churchyard.

The current building is much larger than the original, which was timber-framed and thatched. It has been extended several times, in the 18th, 19th and 20th centuries. Whilst the Bell indisputably has links to smuggling, this did not extend to the storage of contraband. There was no need, because the church was used for this purpose, to such an extent that the sexton of St George on one famous occasion told his rector: "Bain't be no service s'morning parson, Westry be full wi' baccy and pulpit full o' brandy"! The Bell was at one time used almost exclusively by smugglers, who were hostile to anybody outside their group.

The Bell was an institution of some importance during the 19th and early 20th centuries, hosting inquests and regular auctions (notably of farm equipment). It also featured in news reports of 1901, after a rather unsavoury incident. A small group – who had been drinking heavily – left the pub, only for the female member of the party to stagger back to the bar shortly after. She claimed to be feeling unwell, but when she moved her head it was clear that her throat had been cut. Her common-law husband was subsequently tried for attempted murder, but found guilty only of unlawful wounding.

The Bell Inn also features in the novel *The Loves of Joanna Godden* by Sheila Kaye-Smith. A number of sources have reported that the pub has been known in the past as the "stained

---

5. Inns standing within the precincts of parish churches would traditionally be so named to reflect the number of church bells.

The Bell (1950, left; picture: courtesy Kent Messenger) and little changed in 2014

glass window", reflecting its location, but this is not a name that has lasted. It was for a time highly prominent on the hare coursing circuit and still acts as a centre for village activities, with an emphasis on live music and morris dancing. It also holds an annual beer and cider festival.

Newchurch

In the 13th century, when the River Rother flowed out to the sea near Hythe, the now sleepy village of Newchurch was on an island. Until the 1990s, the village had two claims to fame: a church with a leaning spire; and the widely acclaimed Black Bull public house. Sadly, only one remains — and it's not the pub!

In 1943, another of the Marsh Advanced Landing Grounds was constructed on farmland at Newchurch. This and a nearby searchlight battery brought a lot of airmen into the village, most of whom were attracted by the charms of the Black Bull.

Black Bull, Mill Lane, Newchurch, TN29 0DZ

The Black Bull dated back (at least in part) to the reign of Queen Anne and was reputedly built from ships' timbers — a hardly uncommon claim amongst Marsh pubs. It first appears as a pub in *Bagshaw's 1847 Directory*, where William Ovenden is shown as the owner. In its early days it was a popular smugglers' haunt, with a pink-tinted lamp (known colloquially as a strawberry lamp) displayed in an upstairs window to warn free-traders of the presence of revenue officers.

The building is angled away from the road, presumably in a bid to avoid the prevailing winds. It at one time provided the annual suppers (with huge steak pies) for the John Jones

Coursing Club; whilst it has already been demonstrated that some claims to connections with John Jones may be open to question, those for the Black Bull seem *bona fide*.

Described by one source as "the pub of one's dreams", the Black Bull certainly attracted a good press, and even now recalls warm feelings. This is perhaps because it was the archetypal village pub – the secular heart of the village – and was only fully appreciated by some after it had closed. The secret of its success was its lack of pretention. It boasted a games room that catered to most tastes, beer straight from the barrel and basic but excellent food. A staple was its enormous roast-beef sandwiches prepared by the licensee's mother and grandmother (during the 1980s its claim was to serve "the biggest sandwiches you've ever seen") and it was always a treat to witness the huge joints of beef roasting in the Aga.

Basic and unpretentious: this 1980s advert summed up the Black Bull quite nicely

Outside, the pub still advertised stabling for horses as late as 1955. But ironically, it was less able to cater to the needs of more modern transport, and the lack of car parking became a significant problem in its later years. Beneath the inn sign was an unusual (in pub terms) quotation from the Song of Soloman: "I am black but comely . . . as the tents of Keder, as the curtains of Jerusalem".

The Black Bull in its heyday, c. 1950

This photograph of the Black Bull from 1980 illustrates the problems experienced by pubs lacking a dedicated car park

The private house that was once the Black Bull, 2013

Inside, the pub had just two rooms, leading off from a central corridor. At one time, the larger of these was designated as the four-ale bar[6] (subsequently a tap room). Later, one of the rooms was furnished in the manner of a very comfortable living room, and surviving photographs show displays of sporting guns on the walls. A former clubroom upstairs was converted to two bedrooms in the 1970s.

Local legend states that a landlord in the early 20th century – under the influence of his own wares – slipped and fell to his death down the pub well (now long-since boarded over).

---

6. The four-ale bar was traditionally where the cheapest beer was sold (for 4d a quart) and was the forerunner of the public bar.

What is more certain is that the Black Bull was one of a number of Whitbread pubs sold in the 1970s to Shepherd Neame. In the following decade, Shep's sold it on, but it went downhill at the end of the 1980s and many of its customers shifted allegiance to the Shepherd & Crook at Burmarsh. It closed in the mid-1990s.

The building remains but is another now in private ownership.

Old Romney

It is hard to believe that this tiny village (it can't technically be termed a hamlet as it does have its own church) was once a major port, lying on what was formerly an island in the River Rother. The Domesday Book records that Old Romney then had three fisheries, a wharf and a mill. But then, of course, nature took a hand.

Old Romney is now best known for its quintessential Marsh church, the iconic St Clement, "guarded" by its solitary yew tree. Standing defiantly alone, it has been described with some justification as "possibly the most beautiful church in England". It featured in the Disney film version of *Doctor Syn alias the Scarecrow* (with the Disney Corporation contributing to its upkeep) and is now also widely known for its churchyard, which contains the grave of Derek Jarman. Its one pub is separated from the church by the A259 road, which follows the bank of the former Rhee Wall (the channel originally dug to reconnect the port to the sea).

Rose & Crown, Swamp Road, Old Romney, TN29 9SQ

The Rose & Crown dates back to 1689 and was at this time two farm buildings. Then, Old Romney parish comprised just 12 buildings and a church. Trading as a beerhouse prior to 1848, in that year the two buildings were merged and a full licence obtained.

The Rose & Crown was heavily involved with the smuggling trade: in the late 18th century, a report by Thomas Clare, the Hythe Customs Officer, describes the stables as being full of smugglers' horses. He further claims that in the morning he saw:

> 18 men (armed with brass muskatoons, brass fuzees, and pistols) and one boy, all with brazen faces . . . with 60 horses all loaded with dry goods . . . they were such fellows as dare bid Defiance to all Laws and Government.

In common with many of the Marsh pubs, it was for a long time basic and functional — retaining a sanded floor and spittoon up until the late 1940s. And, like many village pubs, it has had unashamedly to widen its horizons to remain viable. 20th century enhancements included the addition of an accommodation block: the Rose & Crown was advertised as a motel in the 1980s but now offers five, more traditional, bedrooms with breakfast provided. In the 1990s, a conservatory was added, which is used primarily by diners. Recent owners have taken a real pride in the appearance of the place and this was manifested in the Rose & Crown being declared Marsh in Bloom winners in both 1999 and 2000.

Top: The Rose & Crown in 1905, showing wooden porches added to the bar and taproom entrances to provide patrons with some protection from the strong Marsh winds. Above: The Rose & Crown pictured in 1980, when it sported a distinctive pink look. The building to the left is the pub's function room. A conservatory has since been added.

Snargate

Yet another tiny Marsh village, Snargate has even fewer chimney pots than its neighbours. Yet it has a number of claims to fame, mostly related to its church. The Reverend Richard Harris Barham, who wrote the acclaimed *Ingoldsby Legends*, was rector here at St Dunstan's for four years in the 19th century. Whilst not himself necessarily involved in the widespread smuggling that took place in the area, he was sympathetic to the smugglers' cause and his church was used for the storage of contraband. The church also sports (in the north aisle) a striking wall painting of a ship, which dates back to 1500. It has been claimed by some historians that this was a coded symbol, indicating that smugglers could find sanctuary here.

Snargate was also home to artist Harold Gilman – the "English van Gogh". Born in 1876, he spent the first 30 years or so of his life in the village: not that surprising, considering that his father (like Barham) was rector here.

Red Lion, A259, Snargate, TN29 9UQ

Despite the history of its church, it is probably the Red Lion that has done most to put Snargate on the map in recent times. Dating from 1540, this two-storey building with white rendered façade was formerly known as the Shepherd & Lamb and once served as a minor coaching inn. It is not known when it became the Red Lion. From the outside, the pub today appears pleasant on the eye but not that remarkable; yet this belies what lies within.

What can one say about the Red Lion that has not been said so many times before? The words "iconic" and "gem" barely do justice to a pub that has been so dominated by its long-serving landlady that it is more commonly known just as "Doris's". And this is not just a name used locally – it is not stretching credibility too far to say that this small, unassuming hostelry on Romney Marsh has a worldwide reputation, and many real-ale *aficionados* undertake regular "pilgrimages" to the establishment.

Doris Jemison used to make shirts in Penge before joining the Land Army and being posted to a farm at Snargate in WWII. She never left! The pub at that time belonged to her future husband, and before that his father, thus remaining in the same family for over a hundred years (from 1911). The couple ran it "just how the men liked it", avoiding any frills and ostentation. When she was widowed in the mid-1980s, Doris pledged to keep it just the same; and no-one could argue that she failed to keep her word. The pub has accordingly remained virtually unchanged since the war. The central bar houses a 200-year-old clock (the dominant ticking of which transports one back to another era), whilst the bar surface itself is an antique

One of the earliest known photographs of the Red Lion, c. 1880

79

"Doris's" pictured in 2014

marble slab. There are also two other rooms, a games room and a back room with piano. All are decorated with WWII memorabilia, and the Land Army features heavily in posters and newspaper cuttings of the time. The handpumps are just for show, as beer is dispensed direct from the barrel. The only food that you will be offered is crisps, other packaged savoury items and pickled onions, but the management is happy for customers to bring their own meals. In one respect, however, modern technology has caught up with the Red Lion: electric lighting has now been installed, although limited to one fitting in each bar, and supplemented by candles in the evening. Famous patrons (who have signed the Visitors' Book) include legendary musicians like Paul McCartney and Lol Crème). Listed in April 1985, it unsuprisingly features in the CAMRA inventory of unspoilt heritage pubs.

It almost goes without saying that there are no jukeboxes or games machines. The Red Lion has, however, proudly maintained its reputation for supporting traditional entertainment. Where else can you still play pre-WWI games such as toad-in-the-hole, shove halfpenny, devil-amongst-the-tailors, shut-the-box and nine men's morris? At one time, skittles, bar billiards and the ancient Kentish game of bat-and-trap were also played here, and the pub was home to a goal-running team.

The games room of the Red Lion, still unchanged in early 2017

You might expect that, with a pub such as this, the toilets would be outside. And you'd be right. Also outside is a wonderful little garden – secluded, but a suntrap at the right time of day. The garden comes complete with free-range chickens and other fowl – again, totally in keeping with the ambience of the pub. A recent innovation has been the holding of a beer festival in the summer, with up to 20 local brews available – on tap, needless to say. As part of this festival, music is staged in the garden. Again, this tends to be low-key and perfectly reflects the image of the place; as does the tradition of the Leeds Society of Handbell Ringers playing tunes here at Christmas.

Sadly, Doris passed away at the end of April 2016. However, after a short period of mourning and closure, Doris's daughter Kate, who has long been involved in the running of the Red Lion, along with her sister Sue, took over the licence. Its future appears to continue to be bright.

St Mary-in-the-Marsh

This is yet another Marsh settlement that essentially comprises a church and a pub. Its two most famous former residents are Edith Nesbit and Sir Noel Coward. Nesbit – best known for writing *The Railway Children* and who had a very unconventional marriage to Hubert Bland – moved here from nearby St Mary's Bay shortly before her death and is buried in the churchyard of St Mary the Virgin, whilst Coward lived in the cottage adjacent to the inn, where he wrote his first successful play. A local guide has said of the village that it is "is surrounded by the stark beauty of the marshes and the open landscapes of rich farmland" and it is hard to better this description. Little has changed over the years.

The church has an unusual weather vane, in that it is mounted upon a ball. Naturally enough, this has proved to be an attractive target for local children, armed with air rifles and other weapons. When maintenance was required in the 1960s, workmen were puzzled to find a nest of bees within the ball, and honey oozing out of a number of bullet holes!

The Star Inn, St Mary-in-the-Marsh, TN29 0BX

The message that the Star puts on its website: "welcome to The Star Inn, where you are a stranger only once" may be clichéd, but it does seem appropriate for this charming white-washed pub. Built in 1476, it qualifies as one of the oldest inns on Romney Marsh. Originally a thatched farm dwelling, it passed through several farming families before being acquired in 1711 by Anthony Jessup, a farmer and brewer, of Ashford. Later that year, Jessup applied for and was granted an ale and cider licence and the house was duly registered as an ale house. At this time it was unnamed but in 1732, after being bought by Thomas Kemp, it acquired its current moniker. This common pub name has its origins in the 11th century, when inns and taverns stood within the precincts of parish churches and many of them were given titles bearing religious meaning. The Star has witnessed and undergone many alterations and been extended over time, but its historic character remains largely unchanged.

The basic simplicity of the Star, 2014

During the 18th century, when tithes were collected from the parish, the rector held tithe suppers at The Star. Easter vestry meetings were also staged here when attendance at the church was thin and, on the odd occasion, the rector would transfer his sermons to the pub! In the 18th and early part of the 19th centuries, fires burned continuously in the pub grate during lambing season as a sign to shepherds tending their flock to come and take shelter at the inn. Many needed no further invitation, often bringing their sick lambs with them.

In more recent years, the Star was a favourite pub for Boxing Day revellers, particularly through the 1960s, when its status as host for the John Jones Hare Coursing Club's Christmas event allowed it to open all day. There is also a local Christmas legend concerning the pot-bellied pig of St Mary-in-the-Marsh, which appears only on Christmas Eve and only to certain pub regulars! Few can now recall the name of the local who inspired this piece of gentle leg-pulling. In the 1980s, the pub was a regular haunt for the actor Dennis Waterman and his then wife, Rula Lenska. In the same decade, it was taken on to the Shepherd Neame estate. An entry in the 1982 guide *Real Ale Pubs in Kent*, which read: "delightful pub with a pleasant garden", still holds true today.

4

Hythe

The town of Hythe was the first of the south-coast ports to be granted a Cinque Ports Charter, back in 1278. But it suffered from the same silting process that afflicted its neighbours, and the harbour gradually became unviable.

Hythe's subsequent development has been shaped by the military and by the construction of the Royal Military Canal (RMC), designed to counter the threat of invasion by Napoleon (indeed, many of the current road names in the town date to this time). But the history of Hythe has also been greatly influenced by two families: the Deedes and the Mackesons. Both have represented the town in parliament and, whilst it is the Mackesons who hold more interest in the context of this book through their brewing empire, the Deedes family (which includes one-time editor of the *Daily Telegraph*, Bill Deedes) also has numerous historical connections with the town's drinking establishments.

The Mackeson brothers' acquisition of the brewery came at an opportune time, when the army had a very real presence and influence. They realised, and soon came to appreciate, that the military brought with them a desire for more than just spiritual refreshment.

The site of the former Mackeson brewery, now home to Mackeson Court (in the Chapel Street/Prospect Road area)

The entrance to Mackeson Court (left); and The Malt House Antiques Market (right) (both 2013)

But in addition to being a major employer, Mackeson's also played a civic role, sponsoring and supporting many local activities and bodies. For example when, during WWII, all reliable horses were commandeered by the army, leaving the Hythe Fire Brigade without transport, it was Mackeson's that stepped in by making one of its brewery lorries available. Whilst brewing on the Hythe site ended in May 1968 (as discussed in Chapter 1), the distribution centre remained in use for a further five years. From the western end of Bartholomew Road and looking down towards Red Lion Square, the "bowl" that you see below you, which now houses a public car park, and the adjoining estate of flats mark the "footprint" of the brewery site. Indeed, the flats have been named Mackeson Court.

An even more tangible reminder of former times can be found in the nearby High Street, where the Malt House has been preserved (but put to alternative use as an antiques market). The old brewery office in the High Street also remains, although this has now been converted into high-quality flats.

More recently (since 2011), Hythe has been served by the Hop Fuzz Brewery. Operating out of the Riverside Industrial Estate in West Hythe and overlooked by Port Lympne Zoo, this is described rather confusingly as a "full-size microbrewery"(!). It has enjoyed considerable success in its short life and supplies numerous pubs both on and beyond the Marsh. Part of its growing popularity lies in its impressive green credentials, which include the use of solar powered pumps throughout the process, recovering and re-using heat, and utilisation of 100% recycled plastic casks. Its vehicles are fuelled by bio-diesel.

In terms of its number of licensed premises in the 19th century, Hythe does not closely follow the national trend. Whilst the quantity did grow significantly as a result of the 1830 Beerhouse Act, there was no major decline following subsequent legislation. Of greater signif-

The premises of the Hop Fuzz Brewery, August 2014

icance in Hythe was the demand created by the army and by those involved in the construction of the RMC. Accordingly, whilst an 1801 directory listed just five pubs in Hythe (all of which were – and are – fine architectural works, and which would each subsequently come under the control of Mackeson), there was a steady growth thereafter and by 1887 there were 19. These were: The Nelson's Head Inn (Bank Street); The New Portland Arms (Bartholomew Street); The Bell (East Street); The Globe, The Oak, The Rose & Crown, The Providence, *The Kings Head*, The Sportsman, *The White Hart*, and *The Swan* (all High Street); *The Red Lion*, Old Portland Arms, *The Duke's Head*, The Gate (all Market Street); The Ordnance Arms (Military Road); The Star and The Hope (Stade Street); and The Three Mariners (Windmill Street).[1] It is similarly not evident that the 1904 police powers had the same impact as, for example, in Rye, even though local temperance campaigners met with local magistrates as early as 1903 to discuss measures to tackle drunkenness. They argued that the 11 pubs in half a mile from the Dukes Head to the Cinque Ports was excessive; but the magistrate countered that only five cases of drunkenness had come before them in the past 18 months. There was a spate of closures later in the century, however, following the demise of the Mackeson brewery; subsequent rationalisation by Whitbread; and the army's closure of the Small Arms School in 1969.

In the early 20th century, a number of roads in the town underwent renumbering. This may cause confusion when former addresses are quoted in public records, particularly where

---

1. Those shown in italics were the original five from 1801.

the High Street (renumbered in 1915) is concerned.[2] Additionally, it should be noted that Market Square has become Red Lion Square, Market Street has become part of Dymchurch Road and some other roads have also undergone a change of name.

Bell Inn, 1 Seabrook Road, Hythe CT21 5NB

(Note – in some sources the address is shown as East Street. East Street runs into Seabrook Road, and the Bell sits right on this border)

Certainly a contender for the title of oldest pub in Hythe, the Bell dates back to the 1500s, when it had a seafront location (and was probably the town's harbour pub). Sources state that it was originally constructed using ships' timbers salvaged from a number of local shipwrecks, although this may just have applied to the outer weatherboarding.

The Bell was also – inevitably – a smugglers' inn, with a tunnel that runs close to the millstream. This was once used as a hiding place for brandy and gin, with contraband being floated up the millstream: when the coast was clear, the items would be hauled up into the inn by means of a windlass – installed in a partitioned portion of the attic – which could be lowered into the water. It is believed that the young son of one of the landlords could get into the stream and wade down to the canal to assist in the collection of such contraband.

Major renovation in the 1960s led to the discovery of an ancient fireplace that contained an assortment of keys, mugs, bones and clay pipes. More significantly, two skeletons wearing boots and hats were found concealed behind the fireplace – and are thought to be those of murder victims.

The Bell in 2012

---

2. Where this is the case, the current number is shown first, with the former number in parentheses.

The Bell is not listed in the Hythe directory of 1801, for the reason that it was then within the parish of Newington (boundaries have since been re-drawn). It would be unusual for a pub of this vintage not to have a resident ghost, and The Bell's is the rather ubiquitous grey lady – a woman who died in childbirth and who now allegedly haunts the cellars.

Britannia Inn, 26 Horn Street, Shorncliffe, Hythe CT21 5SR

Even further outside the main body of Hythe than the Bell is the Britannia Inn, in the hamlet of Shorncliffe. This started life as two adjacent cottages, which predated 1760. For a long time, at least one was (and possibly both were) tied to the Horn Street Mill.

The *Folkestone Chronicle* of September 1859 records both an application for a licence (on the grounds that there was no other pub within half a mile) and its subsequent rejection by the petty sessions bench. Prior to this it probably had an off-sales licence, and was in all likelihood a beerhouse. That much is confirmed by another 1859 *Folkestone Chronicle* article (this time in June) which records the landlord lending assistance to a neighbour whose house was on fire. Whilst he was thus engaged, some soldiers entered "the Britannia ale-house"[3] and forced the elderly landlady to serve them five gallons of beer, for which they refused to pay. They also robbed her of half a pound of tobacco. The miscreants were duly identified and punished, but the incident underlines that the presence of the nearby Shorncliffe garrison has long been significant in the life of the Britannia. Until very recently, it was often the last place in which soldiers drank prior to embarking on tours of duty. The pub name may also have military origins, as it is generally thought to be rooted in the Napoleonic Wars – although for a long time the public bar was adorned with Victorian prints of the Battle of Omdurman.

The Britannia, c1920

---

3. The use of the term "alehouse" was very probably incorrect, indicating that – even at this time – there was confusion over terminology.

The Britannia, 2014

Butt of Sherry, 132 (63) High Street, Hythe CT21 5LD/ 5–7 Theatre Street, CT21 5LA

Sited mostly in Theatre Street but with frontage (now set back) onto the High Street, the Butt of Sherry unusually holds two postal addresses – reflecting that the site formerly accommodated two separate premises.

The history of the Butt's "footprint" is unclear. The bulk of directory references to licensed premises are within Theatre Street, although the street numbers do not always fully accord. *Melville's 1858 Directory of Kent* shows a beer retailer residing in Theatre Street, and *Bagshaw's Directory* shows the same individual was trading in the town at least 11 years earlier. The likelihood is that that the same site was involved, but it can't be categorically shown that this was the same premises in Theatre Street as now. But from the early 1900s onwards there are consistent listings of beer retailers and off licences in this part of the Street, in some years combined with newsagent and tobacconist functions.

There is no record of the High Street part of the site being licensed before WWII (notwithstanding that "refreshment rooms" were listed here in 1932). At the outbreak of war, the site was occupied by a firm of accountants and in 1940 the building was bombed, but fully repaired.

Sources have also suggested that the Butt of Sherry was initially known as the Sherry Butt. Whilst this is plausible, it is difficult to confirm. It is not until 1965 onward that there is a consensus as to events, and it was in this year that planning permission was sought and granted to accommodate a discrete wine bar as part of a new build. This was a brave venture – the first of its kind in Kent – and the owners built an advertising campaign around it. The older building remained intact, although the bulk of it was used as an off licence.

The newly-opened wine bar in 1965 (left; photo: Kent Life) and an advertisement from 1970 still promoting the same venture

The Butt of Sherry was significantly altered when the wine bar was added in 1965 (left – photo courtesy Kent Life); but the building remains instantly recognisable nearly 50 years later (2013)

This dual function remained into the 1970s, although by the time the off licence was discontinued, the main business had arguably reverted to that of a mainstream pub. Although there has been some more recent modernisation – as a result of which the pub now comprises two bars – externally it has changed little in the last 50 years.

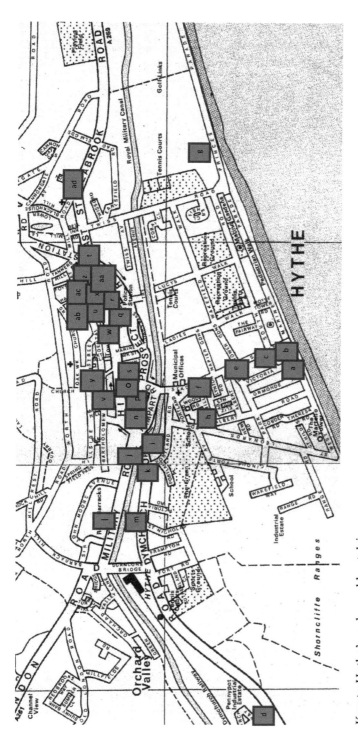

Key to Hythe's pubs and hostelries

a - Stade Court Hotel
b - Hythe Bay Seafood Rest
c - Sutherland House Hotel
d - Prince of Wales
e - Hope Inn
f – Star Inn
g - Mercure Imperial Hotel

h - Three Mariners
i - Red Lion
j - (Old) Portland Arms
k - Duke's Head
l - Ordnance Arms
m - Gate Inn
n - Globe Inn

o - Ordnance Arms
p - Oak Inn
q - Nelson's Head
r - Swan Hotel
s - Butt of Sherry
t - Carousel Lounge
u - White Hart Hotel

v - William Tell
w - Kings Head
x - Providence Inn
y - Prince of Prussia
z - Cinque Ports Arms
aa - Potting Shed
ab - Flying Horse

ac - Sportsman Inn
ad - Bell Inn

Map of Hythe © Philip's; Reproduced by permission of Ordnance Survey on behalf of HMSO. © Crown copyright 100043101. All rights reserved.)

The Carousel Lounge in 2013

Carousel Lounge, 26 Prospect Road, Hythe CT21 5JW

Built for the Loyal Fountain Fellowship lodge in 1903, this building has served a number of different purposes since. In recent years it was a restaurant known as Bentleys, prior to being taken over by the former landlord of the Good Intent at Aldington Frith in March 2008. At this point it was converted into an Art Nouveau style bar. Part of the building remained in use as a restaurant for a short time, converting to a takeaway food business in 2010.

More akin to a hotel lounge bar than a traditional pub, it has built up trade on the back of selling its beer at competitive prices. Whilst not the only Marsh pub to have served beer from their Devizes Brewery, it must be the only one to have displayed a Wadworth's sign.

The Carousel made local news headlines in May 2013, when three councillors undertaking site inspections stumbled across a gang of youths who had stolen a keg of beer and were taking it home in a wheelie bin! The councillors made citizens' arrests and returned the keg to the Carousel, where a press photographer just happened to be waiting.

Cinque Ports Arms, 147 (91) High Street, Hythe CT21 5JN

The Cinque Ports Arms was built in the 17th century, and became one of the first to open as beerhouse under the 1830 legislation. At this time it was known as The Chance.

Always a very small pub, it is much quoted that it was the regular haunt of smugglers and fishermen. Although hardly unique amongst pubs in this area, there is firm evidence that the cellar of the Cinque Ports was regularly used for the storage of contraband. It also had a reputation as a rough pub, and it is said that most locals boycotted it because of this. It is also widely reported that, at one time, the bar sported a stuffed two-headed lamb!

Its size really precluded it being commercially viable in the 20th century and the Cinque Ports Arms closed in March 1961. It is now a solicitor's office.

The Cinque Ports in early 1950s (left) and now catering for an arguably more respectable clientele (2014 – right)

Duke's Head (Inn), 9 Dymchurch Road/Market Street, Hythe CT21 6JB

The Duke's Head stands close to a bridge over the RMC, which bears its name.[4] The original building dates from 1703 and was a dwelling house up until 1749 – when its first licence was granted. At this time it had no name, and operated as a common ale house, from which horse trading was also undertaken. It is yet another Hythe pub with smuggling connections, and rumour has it that a smuggler once hid in the adjacent sewer to evade capture.[5]

In 1750, the pub was sold to the Hythe brewery (John Friend), who in turn sold it in 1801 to William and Henry Mackeson. At this time it was most popular with troops. Shortly after (in 1810) it formally acquired the name the Duke's Head, although right up until the 20th century it was more commonly known as the "Richard, Duke of York" (and the inn sign at one time depicted Wellington!). By 1871, the licensee was operating a carriage business from the inn. The Duke's Head had electric lighting installed in 1906, one of the first in the area to be able to boast this facility. A fire on the premises was recorded in 1932, but no details were provided.

The pub has historically been popular with the farming community, largely because of its location close to the former sheep and cattle market; it would be "heaving" on market days. In Edwardian times, it offered both good stabling and garaging, but this had disappeared by the 1950s, when it provided a greater level of accommodation. This then proved to be a regular

---

4. This was originally the only bridge erected over the canal and was constructed of wood, as all bricks were needed for building the Martello Towers.

5. This is not quite as unpleasant as it sounds: "sewer" is the Marsh term for a drainage ditch.

The Duke's Head, 2013

meeting place for pilots and crew from Silver City Airways (which operated out of Lympne) – who would bring back cans of foreign beers, which would be displayed within the pub.

One of the endearing qualities of Hythe pubs is a reluctance to embroider stories of resident ghosts with historical detail. This could be attributed to laziness, although I personally find it more honest. In the case of the Duke's Head, the occasionally seen apparition is a meek and inoffensive man referred to as "George", who causes no trouble or concern whatsoever.

In 2013 planning permission to convert this listed building into three houses and four flats was refused. However, although it continued to trade for some time after, at the time of writing it is closed and delapidated and a further application for change of use has been submitted.

Changing face of the Duke's Head (1991, far left); and 2013

The Flying Horse, High Street, Hythe

The Flying Horse was sited near the Smuggler's Retreat[6] towards the eastern end of the High Street, and little of its history is recorded. It closed when the licence was transferred to the Seabrook/Imperial Hotel in 1880. It served a number of purposes thereafter, and became a fish shop prior to its demolition in 1908. It occupied the site currently bearing the numbers 81–85.

Gate Inn, 71 Dymchurch Road (Market Street), Hythe CT21 6JN

The Gate was opposite the barracks, on a tollgate of the Hythe–New Romney turnpike (from which, presumably, it took its name). The site was also formerly known as Gallows Corner and the Gate once served as a gaol. Indeed, when still operating as a pub, some of the shackles by which condemned prisoners were manacled to the wall were still visible. For a long time, the inn sign read: "this gate hangs high and hinders none. Refresh and pay, and travel on" (a not uncommon adornment for pubs of this name).

This was another Hythe pub that greatly benefitted from the patronage of troops based in Hythe for the duration of the Napoleonic wars. More unusually, the Gate housed a detachment of the 29th regiment in May 1842, following the wreck of their ship off Dymchurch Wall. A certain amount of notoriety was attracted in 1908 when William Bauldry of Saltwood was arrested here for the murder of his wife. The pub closed in 2011, another victim of the economic downturn.

The Gate (above left) in the 1970s. Now in residential use, the new owners have retained a hanging wooden gate, as shown in 2013

6. The Smugglers Retreat was a much photographed unlicensed 16th century building, with links to the smuggling trade. It was demolished in 1907.

The Globe (pictured in 2013)

The Globe Inn, 6–8 (3) High Street, Hythe CT21 5AT

The Globe is to be found at the top end of the High Street and is close to the RMC. It occupies one of the older surviving buildings in the town, dating back to the late 17th century, and additionally has a small but attractive courtyard garden. For some of its early life it appears to have been a butcher's shop – as it is claimed that the building is haunted by the ghost of a butcher who hanged himself on the premises.

First listed in formal records as a beer shop in 1851, it has been licensed ever since and for much of its existence has earned a reputation as one of the most popular drinking establishments in the town. It retains an open fireplace, exhibits old photographs of bygone Hythe on its walls and regularly hosts live music nights.

Hope Inn, 82 Stade Street, Hythe CT21 6DA

This building dates from around 1790 and was constructed by the army. It provided canteen facilities and officers' quarters for those specifically deployed to counter the Napoleonic threat and the Duke of Wellington stabled his horse here while overseeing the building of the RMC. The army declared it to be surplus to requirements in 1827 and, when it was sold, the new owner successfully applied for a liquor licence. The freehold was bought by Mackeson's in 1885.

The Hope Inn, 2013

This is not the only pub in the area to be named The Hope, although there is some debate as to just who is being commemorated in this instance. Whitbread historians have linked the name to Victor Alexander Hope, Viceroy of India, who was involved in local defence fortifications in Hythe during 1809. Another leading local candidate, however, is Colonel (later Brigadier) Hope, who was heavily involved in the construction of the Martello Towers on this part of the coast.

Some early photos of Hythe depicting the Salvation Army outpost additionally show the Hope's adjacent stables in Albert Lane. For a long time, the pub was in the shadow of the town's windmill, demolished in the late 1870s.

In 1877, a very high tide flooded much of the southern part of the town. As the water entered via Stade Street, the Hope, by virtue of its location, was the most seriously affected of all Hythe's pubs and its occupants had to be rescued from the upstairs windows. Two of the kitchen staff, together with licensee Mrs Sophia Clarke, had been preparing dinner and were amongst the last to make for the higher level; as they reached the stairs they watched their cooker – complete with dinner – float down the street. The tide line from that night remained clearly visible on the outer walls right up until a substantial refurbishment of the pub was undertaken in 1968.

Hythe Bay Seafood Restaurant & Bar

Hythe Bay Seafood Restaurant & Bar, Marine Parade, Hythe CT21 6AW

This site and building have served a number of functions over the years, but since around 2000 this has been a fish restaurant. It is home to the Hythe Bay Seafood Restaurant & Bar, which also more recently opened a sister restaurant at nearby Dover. Its seafront location, with stunning views across the channel, is a huge selling point. As its name implies, it houses a discrete bar and a large outside seating area, which is very popular during the summer months.

King's Head, 117 (106) High Street, Hythe CT21 5JJ

Most historians agree that this old coaching inn is the longest continuously trading pub in the town, having served the thirsty of Hythe since 1513. Until 1584, it was known as the George (after the patron saint) and in 1714 as the Sun before acquiring its current name in 1750. It is the only inn mentioned in the town's famous "Gleanings from the Minute Books".

Whilst still trading as the George, it hosted a sumptuous feast for members of the Town Council celebrating the election of Oliver Cromwell as Lord Protector in 1653. In more recent times, Shepherd Neame purchased the freehold in February 1977, while local MP Michael Howard pulled pints here to raise money for the Royal British Legion in 2003. The interior of the pub has been modernised (rather unsympathetically in some eyes), but the iron

The King's Head (top left) c. 1950 (photo David Harper). Whilst The King's Head sign has previously depicted Charles II, it currently commemorates Henry VIII – in whose reign it was first licensed. (Pictures both 2014)

posts supporting the ceiling indicate that it once comprised several bars. But, being a low beamed building with a number of open fires, it has retained much of its charm. Further, it still possesses a rather unusual and pleasing roof garden.

Any self-respecting building of this vintage has to have a secret passage and/or a resident ghost. The King's Head is no exception, boasting a secret meeting room with small sliding door and the lingering presence of former serving maid Catherine Scothers. Poor Catherine died in unfortunate circumstances in 1897, but is said to be responsible for the opening of doors, even when they have been locked and bolted!

Mercure Hythe Imperial Hotel (Seabrook Hotel), Princes Parade, Hythe CT21 6AE

This imposing building which backs onto the Hythe Imperial Golf Club was constructed by and for the South Eastern Railway and opened in July 1880 at the end of the sea front on Princes Parade, on the site of former Martello Tower no.10. It was part of the proposed Seabrook Estate – which was to include very exclusive housing and even a pleasure pier – and was built in the expectation of a rail link being established between Hythe and Folkestone. No expense was spared, and it cost £30k – a fortune at this time. The alcohol licence was transferred from the Flying Horse in the High Street.

*The Imperial Hotel in 1920;
and the Mercure (2013)*

None of the other planned development materialised, however, so the Seabrook Hotel (as it was then known) was never able to fulfil its potential. Understandably struggling financially, in 1901 it was sold and became the Imperial Hotel. In 1946 it was acquired by WJ Marston & Son (who also owned the Stade Court Hotel) and then underwent further baffling cosmetic name changes (from Hotel Imperial at Hythe to Hythe Imperial Hotel [!]) until its sale to Mercure in 2008. In 2011, the windows and roof were substantially repaired, and its colour scheme changed to grey. Set in four acres of land and with enviable views across the channel, it now offers over 100 en suite bedrooms, spa, leisure club, restaurants and bars; and is licensed for civil ceremonies. It also has its own nine-hole golf course.

The Mercure received unwanted press attention in September 2012 when armed police were called after a man threatened a member of staff with a gun.

Nelson's Head Inn, 1–3 Prospect Road,[7] Hythe CT21 5NS

The Nelson's Head stood close to the site of the former Shoemaker's Bridge, which crossed a stream that was subsequently obliterated with the construction of the RMC. It was for this association that the pub was initially known as the Shoemakers Arms (although it is unclear if this was ever its formal name). There are references to the Nelson's Head from the 1840s onwards.

The pub's inn sign has long fostered (incorrect!) speculation as to the origin of its name. A sign first hung in 1938 depicted Lord Nelson, although it was soon pointed out that the eye-patch covered the wrong eye and that his greatcoat was the wrong colour. In 1966 – some 28 years later – these inaccuracies were finally addressed! But both signs ignore a rather more mundane reality: that the pub acquired its name through years of ownership by the local Nelson family; and there is no suggestion that there was any tangible connection to the erstwhile Admiral of the Fleet.

This advert from the 1970s demonstrates that the pub was happy to trade on its non-existent heritage! Despite the pub sign having corrected this error, this advert depicts Admiral Nelson with an eyepatch over his good eye (whilst Nelson lost the sight of his right eye in battle, it is anyway widely questioned whether he regularly wore an eyepatch)

---

7. Prospect Road was formerly Bank Street; and at one time the Nelson's address also appeared as Shoemaker's Bridge Place.

The Nelson's Head (left) in the 1960s (photo: David Harper) and (below) Southern Spice, the business now occupying the much-changed building

During WWII, Hythe suffered some severe bombing and the Nelson's Head seems to have borne more than its fair share. In August 1942, a decorator painting the exterior of the pub was killed by a blast; and in the 1960s, excavations aimed at identifying the source of a long-standing drainage problem uncovered an unexploded bomb, which had to be diffused by the Army. During the same decade, an audit undertaken by landlords Mackeson identified that they had been heavily subsidising a premium bond scheme operated by the landlord.

The Nelson's Head unfortunately became a victim of both Hythe's over-crowded pub market and the military evacuation, and closed in October 1974. Reopening soon after as a restaurant – the Nelson Griddle – it was subsequently taken over by well-known local businessman, Carlos Sotirio. He renamed it Sotirio's Restaurant and traded successfully for 21 years. In 2013, however, he moved his operation to larger premises in Greatstone.[8]

---

8. See Chapter 2.

Ordnance Arms in c. 1950

Ordnance Arms, 1 Military Road, Hythe CT21 5DD

In existence by 1843, the local press records one of the Ordnance Arms' landlords being subject to bankruptcy proceedings in 1876. Sited close to the Small Arms School, it survived the war but closed some time before 1973, when it was demolished to make way for a petrol station. The photograph shows part of the adjacent Military Terrace (left), which still exists in the same form today.

(Old) Portland Arms, Market Street, Hythe

Nestling between the Red Lion and Duke's Head, the earliest mention of the Portland Arms is in 1855. It also appears in the 1871 census, where the landlord is identified as a "beerhouse keeper". The links to Mackeson's (see entry under the Prince of Prussia) suggest a rather more significant operation than a simple beerhouse. Although trading records are incomplete,

Drawing of the (Old) Portland Arms

it seems that the Old Portland Arms was operating at least until 1903. It had certainly stopped by 1906, when it went up for sale by auction. The image shown, by a local artist, post-dates 1875, as it was at this time that the "Old" prefix was added.

Prince of Prussia Inn/New Portland Arms, Bartholomew Street (corner of Three Posts Lane)[9] CT21 5ED

This large Grade II listed building is located on the south side of Bartholomew Street, and was constructed around 1859. It was part of the larger property now known as "Brewery Buildings". At this time its principal function was probably as a lodging house (used mostly by officers attending the School of Musketry), and records show that it was offering 16 rooms in 1861.

By 1868 – when its landlord was implicated in a court case – it was trading as a fully licensed public house and soon after (in 1875) it changed its name from the Prince of Prussia to the New Portland Arms. The Prussian empire was expanding greatly at this time and was causing concern in much of Europe; accordingly the change of name may have been in part to avoid negative public feeling. The *raison d'etre* of the new name is easier to deduce according to local histories, as Mackeson's (who owned it) also owned the (Old) Portland Arms.

This establishment appears in the 1891 census as Brewery Buildings for the first time, making it likely that the New Portland Arms had closed as a pub earlier that year. From this time it reverted to its former use as lodgings, and for students of brewing history, it may be of interest that it was thereafter regularly used in this capacity by employees of the nearby Mackeson's brewery. The building was sold in 1985 and converted into three flats. It retains its Brewery Buildings signage.

Brewery Buildings in 2013

---

9.   Prior to the 1850s, Bartholomew Street was known both as Back Road and Elm Terrace.

The Potting Shed, 160a High Street, Hythe CT21 5JR

The Potting Shed was formally opened by MP Damien Collins in September 2014. This may be one of the more significant developments, as it was the first micropub to appear on the Marsh.

The micropub is a modern concept affair, first seen in 2005.[10] It is essentially a small free house that has real ale at its core, encourages conversation as the main form of entertainment and – if dabbling in any food at all – serves only traditional pub snacks. Many serve their beer straight from the cask and some do not even have a bar. The Potting Shed is fairly representative of the genre, in that it is a converted café/bistro. The management team has experience of Marsh pubs and has vowed to listen to the wishes of the patrons in terms of opening hours and even future direction. Places such as this may hold the key to the future pub landscape.

Prince of Wales, Dymchurch Road, Hythe CT21 6NB

On the border of Hythe and the small community of Palmarsh, this building started life as a beerhouse trading as The Surprise (and it is first mentioned as such within the 1858 *London Gazette*), but by 1874 it had become the Prince of Wales. It shares with the Pilot (Lydd-on-Sea) the distinction of having had a station halt on the RH&DR named after it. But whilst the Pilot Halt enjoyed some popularity, the Prince of Wales' counterpart was less successful. Timetabled as a request halt for the first year of the railway's service, it had no platform or station buildings; and it has even been claimed that no passenger ever boarded or alighted here!

For many years known as a popular bikers' pub, from the turn of the 21st century the Prince of Wales underwent a number of changes of ownership and landlords; never a good sign. It has had spells of closure and whilst planning permission has been sought for conversion to residential use at various times, its sale by Enterprise Inns in 2014 means that it has become a free house. Although it was feared that the RH&DR's Prince of Wales bridge could become the only reminder of the pub's existence, it seems that the pub does now have a future.

---

10. The passing of the 2003 Licensing Act – which came into effect two years later – facilitated the establishment of small independent public houses. The first such micropub was in Herne, Kent.

The Prince of Wales, pictured in 2013, between owners

The Providence, 143 (93) High Street, Hythe CT21 5JL

It seems that The Providence was initially a beerhouse of some size, additionally occupying (what are now) the adjoining premises at number 143a. By 1898 it had become a fully fledged public house serviced by Finn's Lydd brewery. It enjoyed some success for a short time, but closed its doors in 1911. The premises were subsequently taken on by a fruiterers and continued to serve Hythe in this capacity up until 1982.

Red Lion, Red Lion Square, Hythe CT21 5AU

This former coaching inn standing opposite the old Mackeson Brewery dates back at least to 1670 and was once the most important of all Hythe's buildings, giving its name to the square in which it stands. It was initially known as the Watersedge, and then for much of its early life as the Three Mariners, before becoming established as the Red Lion.

Undoubtedly a smugglers' inn at one time, the Red Lion more latterly developed trade around transport, first as a stop or destination on the stagecoach route. Later it performed a similar function for tram and bus services, with The Folkestone, Sandgate and Hythe Tramways Company erecting a tram shed in Red Lion Square in 1894.[11] There have inevitably been structural changes over the years, and the stables have long been converted into garages and a

---

11. This closed in 1922.

The Red Lion in 2012

small garden. But the main fabric of the building has changed little and remains instantly recognisable. Until relatively recently, an ostler's bell remained *in situ* as a reminder of the Red Lion's coaching house past. And, inside, you will still find many reminders of its Mackeson's connection.

In fiction, the Red Lion was a regular haunt of Mr Mipps, sidekick of Russell Thorndike's smuggling vicar Dr Syn. It is also claimed to be haunted by the ghost of a deceased tram driver who was badly injured by falling masonry after a wartime bomb had wreaked havoc. He was carried into the bar, where he died from his wounds.

In 2000, in an attempt to change its image, it reverted to its earlier name of the Watersedge. Part of this "re-badging" involved signage featuring a canal barge. The move was deeply unpopular, and critics pointed out that the RMC had never utilised the type of boat depicted! Local pressure resulted in the change back to the Red Lion in 2005.

Rose & Crown, 38 (17) High Street, Hythe CT21 5AT

Mentioned in *Bagshaw's 1847 Directory*, it is highly likely that the Rose & Crown existed as a beerhouse before this time. The building – timber framed and re-fronted in the 18th century – certainly predates this. At some point it took over an adjoining butcher's shop and possibly another property.[12]

---

12. This row of properties has been subject to change over the years; when number 38 was afforded Grade II listed building status in 1973, numbers 38a and 40 were treated similarly.

Pictorial representation of the Rose & Crown c.1860 (left); and as Thailand Tom's in 2014 (right)

Records that do exist paint an interesting picture of social conditions in this part of Hythe in the 1870s. The landlord additionally owned a row of cottages sited between the High Street and Chapel Street, which were known as "Rose & Crown Cottages" and which were let to tramps and travellers. These were amongst the worst slums in the town, and at the end of the row were pigsties and an open privy. After much public concern had been expressed, these cottages were demolished in 1931. In later years, the pub was yet another to suffer from the military evacuation of the town. It closed in 1971, when it became a fruit shop. But it later re-opened as licensed premises, under several different names (including **Earl Brown's**, **Carriages Tavern** and **Carriage's Wine Bar**). It closed again in 2008 but, after remaining empty and boarded up for a considerable time, the premises now house a successful restaurant – Thailand Tom's.

The Sportsman Inn, 107 (111) High Street, Hythe CT21 5JH

The Sportsman – opposite the entrance to Market Street on the north side of the High Street – had only a relatively brief existence, but a spectacular demise.

Listed as a beershop in *Melville's 1858 Directory*, records of landlords commence in the same year and it is unlikely to have opened much before then. Located very close to four other pubs, competition was fierce, and this was behind a move by the police to close it down in 1905. The Sportsman survived this, but not a disastrous fire that broke out two years later, in June 1907, when the landlord and his wife were away. The local fire brigade attended but by this time it had taken such a hold that their efforts concentrated only on trying to prevent its spreading to adjacent shops.

The spectacle drew huge crowds, and the Sportsman was gutted. Many attending declared that this was the best entertainment seen in Hythe for a long time! So it was perhaps only fitting that the new building erected on the site (and opened in 1911) was a cinema – the Hythe Picture Palace. The cinema, however, lasted only 16 years before being demolished. The site is now home to a florist's shop.

Aftermath of the fire that gutted the Sportsman Inn in 1907

Star Inn, 48 Stade Street,[13] Hythe CT21 6BD

Despite trading for over 150 years, the Star seems to have led a pretty uneventful existence. First listed in 1855, very little of its history has been recorded. Unusually for a Romney Marsh pub, it does not even have any claimed links to the smuggling trade; ironic in view of the fact

The former Star public house, pictured in 2014

---

13. Stade Street has been renumbered in parts and this was formerly – in all likelihood – number 37. The current number is shown as 42 by some sources, which is incorrect.

that a descendant of the Roaring Ransleys – Frank Ransley – was publican from 1930 to 1937. He hanged himself after going off duty one Christmas lunchtime, fearful that his mismanagement of the pub's Thrift Club was about to be uncovered.

Located on the corner of Stade Street and Windmill Street, the Star very much resembled its near neighbour the Three Mariners (after the latter expanded). In the 1970s it earned a reputation as a popular back-street "local" and hosted successful darts teams. It closed in 1981 and is now an unremarkable private house.

Stade Court Hotel, Stade Street, West Parade, Hythe CT21 6DT

Commanding excellent sea views, the Stade Court was built around 1939, on the site of a number of small cottages. Now part of the Best Western chain, its bars and restaurant have long been open to non-residents.

The entrance to the right of the Stade Court was once to a ground floor restaurant, Dr Syn's Parlour. The white block to the right is the site of the former Sutherland House Hotel

Sutherland House Hotel, 126 Stade Street, Hythe CT21 6DY

Probably dating from the late 19th century, the first recorded reference to the Sutherland Boarding House (as it was then known) is within a newspaper report of 1899 – recording the sad suicide of a French woman who was lodging there.

The name was taken from the nearby Sutherland Fort, sited in the Hythe Rifle Ranges. The hotel was partly demolished and converted to flats and garages in 1981.

Sutherland House Hotel at the end of the 1950s (left); and the flats now standing on its site (below)

Swan Hotel/Swan Commercial Inn, Family Hotel & Posting House, 59 (131) High Street, Hythe CT28 5AD

The Swan Hotel was first mentioned in 1506, and was later a popular coaching inn. Confirming its credentials, a milestone in the wall shows that it is 12 miles from Ashford and 71 from the capital. Another notable sign on the wall, which is still visible, is the Sun Insurance plate. This dates from the days when a fire would be tackled only if the householder had insured his premises with the appropriate company.

Although there is no record of fire at the Swan, in the early hours one Sunday morning in 1884, there was a famous incident in Bartholomew Street, just behind the hotel. Here stood three old cottages, mainly of wooden construction. When a fire took hold here, one of the residents ran to the Swan to raise the alarm and, whilst her prompt action managed to protect the neighbouring properties (including the Swan), one person was burned to death in his bed.

By the 18th century, the Swan was one of the top inns in the county; and both Tsar Alexander of Russia and, later when passing through Kent in 1814, the Duchess of Oldenburg took tea there with Mayor Richard Shipdem.

In addition to the coaching trade, the Swan was heavily involved with other forms of transport. In 1807 it launched a packet-boat service to Appledore on the RMC. A daily service ran right up until 1851, when the advent of the Ashford–Hastings railway rendered it no longer viable. Later, in the 1870s, proprietor Henry Ovenden ran one of three

horse-bus businesses operating out of Hythe. Rather strangely, in the middle of the same century, the Swan was additionally housing a tax office, a posting house, a small corn market and a gentlemen's club. It features as the Ram's Head in *The House in Paris*, the acclaimed 1935 novel by Irish novelist Elizabethan Bowen. Its central position ensures that the Swan today retains some significance within the town.

The Swan has changed little from the 1970s (left) to the present day (right)

Three Mariners, 37 Windmill Street, Hythe CT21 6BH

As previously indicated, Hythe has accommodates two establishments by the name of the Three Mariners (the Red Lion formerly trading as such). But it is the distinctive inn sign of this pub that catches the eye, as it shows only one figure. It celebrates the elderly naval man in W. S. Gilbert's *The Yarn of the Nancy Bell*, one of his *Bab Ballads* – who was a "cook and a captain bold, and the mate of the Nancy Brig". The name reflects the fact that, after being shipwrecked, the mate had eaten his two shipmates (according to the ballad, it was more than two). The portrait on the sign is copied from Gilbert's own illustration of his verse. This image was also in use when Whitbread commissioned its reproduction inn sign series in 1951. At one time, however, the pub's sign depicted three giants of the seafaring world: Sir Walter Raleigh, Sir Francis Drake and Captain James Cook.

This modest back-street pub was built in the mid-19th century and in operation by 1874. For a long time it was the smallest pub in Hythe until Mackeson's (in 1936) purchased the property next door[14] in order to enlarge it. Another point of interest is that it at one time had an entrance via an up-and-over garage door. Later under the ownership of Whitbread, the Three Mariners was purchased by Shepherd Neame in May 1975 but was sold and refurbished, becoming a free house, in 2007. Unusually for the time, it declared itself to be a "wet" pub only, declining to augment its income by serving food. With no jukebox, fruit machine or pool table, it soon became a mecca for the real-ale fraternity as well as its loyal locals, and was acknowledged by CAMRA. In awarding the Three Mariners second place in their local pub of the year awards in 2010, it said: "(this) traditional 2-bar back-street local is a jewel in the crown". The policy on food and electronic noise remains in force.

The impressive Three Mariners and its intriguing sign, pictured in 2012

White Hart (Hotel), 71 High Street, Hythe CT21 5AJ

Whilst the King's Head is in all likelihood the oldest pub in Hythe, the White Hart – the principal inn of Hythe – certainly has a long history, and has laid claim to the unofficial title. Although Whitbread date it to 1648 and other sources to the 15th century, a building was

---

14. 35 Windmill Street, formerly Wilkins' Baker's shop.

probably first constructed on this site in 1395. There are further claims that a dwelling existed here in 1290, but that this was destroyed by fire. The subsequent building was probably destroyed in 1580, by the earthquake that also accounted for part of Saltwood Castle. There is nothing of the earlier buildings within the current exterior, which has undergone extensive alteration over the years, particularly in the late 17th century (when the present façade was erected) and again the following century. However, it is believed that parts of the earlier buildings have survived internally.

It was in 1475 that a licence was granted (to a fisherman from Folkestone) and the property became first registered under its current name. At this time, however, it was spelled "Whytte Harte", later still becoming the "Whyte Hearte". Historian John Kett considers that the inn's name comes from the shape of the headdress worn by the lay sisters who had administered to the pilgrims passing through Hythe; although most consider that the white hart, a symbol of King Richard II (1377–99) may well have been the real inspiration – and this would also support arguments for a 14th century origin.

By the mid-1500s, it had become a thriving inn and, under new regulations (the Act of 1552), the house was granted a wine licence. By the early 1600s, the Mayor and Jurats of Hythe had taken to assembling at the inn, and dined here after electing new members of parliament for the port. By 1670, the White Hart was considered to be an inn of importance, evidenced by the fact that in this year John Bassett was granted the right to issue his own trade tokens.[15] In common with his father, John Bassett went on to become Mayor of Hythe (as, subsequently, did other members of the family). The White Hart remained in the hands of the Bassetts until 1733, when it came into the possession of one of the Deedes family – Julius. Julius Deedes was an interesting character and features prominently within histories of Hythe.

The courtyard and interior of the White Hart, pictured in the 1950s

---

15. These tokens arose from the shortage of minted coins in the 17th century: one side bore the name and sign of the inn whilst the reverse that of its keeper.

He would also become mayor, although his tenure was marked by controversy, and his life was a colourful one. Deedes owned a malt-house at nearby Newington, so may have brewed his own beer here; and the White Hart would remain in the family for many generations. In 1794, the present town hall adjoining the inn was constructed and, during the course of this, a connecting doorway was made between the upper floor of the inn and the lobby of the council chamber, which survives to this day. This enabled the Mayor to use one of the rooms as a robing chamber, for which the inn charged a small fee.

At some point around the late 18th/early 19th centuries, the White Hart became a posting house, serving the London stage. Advertised as a "commercial and posting inn", it offered the luxury of hip baths and showers. Famous guests at this time included the civil engineer John Rennie. Rennie, who had built the Waterloo, Southwark and London bridges, became more locally involved as a consulting engineer on both the RMC and the reconstruction of the Dymchurch sea wall and held planning meetings involving both William Pitt and the Duke of Wellington at the White Hart.

In June 1806, when the Archbishop of Canterbury was a guest, fire again struck – destroying much of the stables. Two of the Archbishop's six horses died and another was so badly burnt it had to be destroyed. A fourth was scorched but believed to have survived.

By 1860, the inn had become the White Hart Commercial Inn and Family Hotel. In the 1930s, it became another favoured venue for pilots undertaking international flights from nearby Lympne Airport. These included Jim Mollison and Tommy Rose, who stayed in the hotel prior to making their record-breaking flight to Cape Town; Charles Scott, who flew to Australia; and Jean Batten (to New Zealand). The White Hart remained open throughout

The White Hart Hotel, in 2013

WWII, welcoming and entertaining servicemen. Bader, Montgomery and American Ambassador John Winant all stayed overnight; less welcome would have been the three soldiers who stole bottles of whiskey (they were subsequently apprehended and each fined the sum of £2). During the 1950s and 1960s, the Irish novelist Elizabeth Bowen used to stay and entertain here and (as with the Swan) described the White Hart for posterity in one of her works.

Also worthy of note are the beautifully turned oak staircase, the fine early 19th century casting of the Royal Arms behind an open hearth, some items of antique furniture that have known no life outside the premises, and a priest's hole. Despite closing in 2008, the White Hart re-opened soon after, and still accommodates at least two harmless ghosts. It is now also the unofficial brewery tap for the nearby Hop Fuzz Brewery.

Other Hythe pubs

Those other Hythe pubs and beerhouses of which there is only limited information available and which are no longer with us include:

- Flix (formerly Jams), Marine Parade – this was a short-lived seafront pub and nightclub, popular with the young. On the site of the current Hythe Bay Seafood Restaurant, its heyday was in the 1990s.
- Nag's Head, Market Street – *Melville's 1858 Directory* records a beershop of this name in 1858, but no other detail.
- Oak Inn, 22 (10) High Street CT21 5JU – first recorded in 1887, the Oak may well have been established prior to this. Still trading after WWII, in 1949 the wife of the licensee was tried for receiving stolen goods (belonging to the War Department), but acquitted. In the 1980s it became a stamp dealer's shop, before reverting to licensed premises in the form of (first) Raquets Wine Bar and then Pancho's Cantina Bar. It is now an Italian restaurant.
- William Tell, Bartholomew Street – first mentioned in 1855, the William Tell also appears in *Melville's 1858 Directory* and *London Gazette* court records of the same year. The latter account relates that James Driscoll – "formerly of the Nags Head" – was sued over a trading dispute. Given the nature of the Nag's Head, it is likely that the William Tell was also a beershop.

The former Oak Inn, pictured in 2014

West Hythe

Today, there is no pub at West Hythe,[16] which is an unremarkable village/"suburb" of Hythe. The small Riverside Industrial Estate (which houses the Hop Fuzz Brewery – see Hythe main narrative) is the main development of note. Yet West Hythe was not always so quiet, and has enjoyed a rich history. Nearby was the Roman port of Portus Lemanis, and the remains of this are still visible. West Hythe had its own church, first mentioned in 1089. This was rebuilt in the 12th century and extended in the 13th. But by the mid-16th century, the settlement had dwindled to just four households and the church fallen into disrepair. In 1620 the church was further damaged by fire.

As with Hythe itself, the building of the RMC stimulated the economy, and the number of houses increased. Some of these were along the West Hythe Road/Lympne Hill (which has further developed since) but more were built in St Mary's Road. "Road" is something of a misnomer – it is a no-through lane, not denoted on all modern maps; it is to be found just to the north of the RMC, heading east, and does not currently display its name. There are still a number of houses along here, as well as the somewhat impressive remains of the afore-mentioned church. And it was St Mary's Road that (most probably) hosted both of West Hythe's pubs.

Carpenters' Arms, St Mary's Road, West Hythe CT21 4NU

On the north bank of the RMC, census evidence shows that the Carpenters' Arms was operating by 1841. One of the first licensees listed was additionally credited as being a shepherd, which gives a good indication of both the size of the operation and the rural nature of West Hythe at this time.

The Carpenters' Arms, early 20th century (left) and 2015 (right)

---

16. Although the Botolphs Bridge Inn also has a West Hythe postal address, Botolphs Bridge is considered as a hamlet in itself and is treated as such within this book; see Chapter 3.

Adverts in the *Folkestone, Hythe, Sandgate and Cheriton Herald* encouraged the public to take a rowing boat to visit the pub, which also offered good fishing from its banks. The landlord was widowed in 1915 when his wife died of cirrhosis of the liver, at the age of just 43. The Carpenters' Arms is mentioned in a number of autobiographies of local people, often as a place where juveniles could drink without having to answer too many questions, although in 1918 the landlord was fined for not complying with the terms of his licence. Some histories assume that it closed at the outbreak of WWII, but it struggled on for a good few years after, and was still listed in directories in the 1960s. The building still stands, only slightly modified, although vegetation has largely obscured the view from the south. It now bears the name St Mary's House.

Great Gun

As with numerous long-gone pubs, details of the Great Gun are sketchy. There is nothing to indicate that it existed prior to 1801, but it had certainly opened for business by 1805 — strongly suggesting that it was to fulfil yet further need arising from work on the RMC. An inquest into the death of Burmarsh man George Moss opened here in 1806, but was subsequently transferred to the new Guildhall; and this is the last surviving reference to the pub. Although there is no conclusive proof that it was sited in St Mary's Road, references strongly suggest that this was the case.

5

Rye

The name Rye is derived from a Saxon word for island, for at one time the town was almost completely surrounded by the sea. Because it is such an enclosed settlement, the picturesque and historic settlement of Rye provides a very interesting case study of the way in which pubs have been regulated over the years. As one of the chief ports of England in mediaeval times, it would have had many inns and ale houses open in 1300 – but nearly all were destroyed when the town was subject to one of the increasingly frequent French raiding parties, in 1377. Rye was burnt almost to the ground, only the very few buildings of stone construction surviving in any form. Whilst this event led to the serious fortification of the town, the harbour eventually lost its unequal battle with nature and – as a result of silting and the receding of the sea – Rye's fortunes as a port declined.

One of a number of things that sets Rye apart from other Marsh towns and villages is the wealth of its historical records. There are many good and detailed histories available covering various aspects of Rye's development, and two books deal specifically with its pubs and inns: *Old Inns & Ale-Houses of Rye* (1965) by Geoffrey Bagley (published by Rye Museum); and the excellent and more authoritative *The Pubs of Rye, East Sussex 1750–1950* (2012) by David Russell (publised by Lynda Russell). Nonetheless, not all sources are in full agreement over dates and events.

In 1574, the first reliable records show that Rye had some 26 inns and alehouses. The legislation brought in to try to regulate their influence was clearly not particularly successful in Rye as, in 1581, magistrates saw fit to ban some "12 common drunkards" from all alehouses in Rye. Subsequently, the number of licensed premises fluctuated quite alarmingly. At the start of the 17th century there were as many as 40; by 1772 the number had dwindled to six; and by 1815 to just four. The 1830 Beer Act had a huge impact, with the number rising back up to 22 by 1839 and 32 by 1872. But within two years of the passing of new legislation, the number had fallen back to 21 (in 1874). The temperance movement gathered strength in Rye around this time, and may have influenced the police in using their powers under the 1904 Licensing Act to successfully recommend the closure of as many as eight pubs between 1904 and 1911. In more recent times, there was a post-war peak of 21 pubs in 1974, and the current number is around six fewer.[1] But the closure of some of Rye's licensed establishments

---

1. All figures should be treated with some caution as definitions and town boundaries have changed over time.

should not necessarily be treated with any great sorrow: for what most consider now to be a very genteel little town, Rye has had a significant number of seedy and very rough beerhouses and pubs and, in current parlance, the police were "very well acquainted" with many.

A major incident involving its pubs rocked Rye in 1852 – this was known as the "treating scandal". The backdrop was the general election of that year, and the campaign of the victorious Liberal Alexander McKinnon was marked by the (equally!) liberal and totally illegal hosting of drinking sessions in return for votes. Some 20 pubs and beerhouses were implicated in a Parliamentary Report (it would surely have been easier to name those not so involved) and no less a person than the town mayor was imprisoned as a result. Some of today's politicians would surely be proud!

Although very self-contained and traditional, Rye has undergone numerous changes over the years, including the renaming of some of its streets. Notably, the current High Street was formerly Longer Street (for quite logical reasons!) whilst Market Street was once known as the Butchery; Mermaid Street previously as Middle Street; and Landgate as King Street. Accordingly, the addresses of some of Rye's pubs have changed over time.

Bowen's Landgate/Eagle Brewery, Landgate TN31 7LH

When operated by James Batchelor in the 1850s, this was only a small affair, but expanded quickly when purchased by John Bowen[2] later in the century. From this point on it was known as Bowen's Landgate Brewery, but subsequently became the Eagle Brewery (whilst continuing to brew beers that bore the Bowen name). The site remained in use as a brewery and distribution centre when acquired by Alfred Leney and Co. of Dover in 1896, until its disposal at auction in 1923. The yard was in King Street, almost opposite the Queen's Head, and the estate comprised a number of different units. Since closure, parts of the estate have been put to various different uses, serving as removals warehouse, showroom, storage, office accommodation, and as Rye Royal British Legion HQ. In late 2005, planning permission was granted to demolish the former brewery and seven flats were constructed on that part of the site. However, there are still plenty of reminders of the former brewing operations: Eagle

House remains as a listed building with façade intact, but has been extended at the rear and sub-divided into offices and flats; and the stables also still exist (as garages). The Brewery Yard Club (11 Landgate) – a sports and social club – is based in the yard, having taken over from the British Legion, and the thoroughfare between here and Rope Walk is named Eagle Road, recalling the brewery name.

---

2.   Both Batchelor and Bowen also had interests in pubs within the town, the latter building up quite a portfolio.

The Eagle Brewery site today. Clockwise (from top left): new flats on the site; former stables / garages; the Brewery Yard Club; and Eagle House (all 2014)

East Guldeford/Chapmans Brewery, Military Road, Rye TN31 7NY

East Guldeford Brewery, sited to the east of the town on the banks of the River Rother adjacent to the Military Road (and just within the parish of East Guldeford) was established by the Lamb Family in the 18th century. Later on it was taken over by Herbert Verrell Chapman, a major "player" in the Rye drinking scene, who was also a wine and spirit merchant with both High Street and Lydd addresses. Subsequently, his enterprises were registered under the name of Chapman Brothers,[3] although little is known about his brother(s). But by the 1880s, Chapman Brothers owned at least six licensed houses in the town, including the Globe, Greyhound, Tower, Ferry Boat, and London Stout House. Their best known products were Rye Milk Punch and Romney Marsh Sloe Gin, both advertised as winter beverages.

In the face of the competition that arrived with the railway network, its out-of-the-way location counted against the brewery, and it closed in 1911. Most of the brewery was demol-

---

3. For a short time prior to this Chapman was in another commercial partnership, trading as Chapman and Elliot.

ished when it closed, although a part of the building still remains – incorporated within the Rye Lawn Tennis Club.[4] Much of the Chapman Brothers' estate was later (in 1920) bought up by Finn's.

Meryon/Meryon & Holloway Brewery, Strand, Rye TN31 7DH

The Meryon family (fierce rivals of the Lambs) was also instrumental in forging Rye's history, with Lewis Meryon a major influence in the licensed trade. In addition to the George Hotel, Red Lyon and Kings Head, he owned a brewery in the Strand/Wish Ward area of the town. When he died in 1824, the brewery was the principal asset of a significant estate. John Meryon took over the concern and later persuaded his brother-in-law William Holloway to enter the business. This in itself was a rather unlikely alliance, with Holloway being a failed farmer, but the joint venture was for a time a great success and by 1839 was known as Meryon & Holloway. By the time of Holloway's death in the 1850s, however, the partnership had been dissolved and the brewery had joined the list of his failed businesses.

The Meryon Brewery building can still be seen today (occupied by Rye Tiles), and sports a tablet bearing the initials of Lewis Meryon, with the date 1802

Other brewers

Other Rye breweries/brewers about which less is known include the Albion Brewery, the Bull Head Malthouse and Hodges & Ritchie. Of these, the Albion would appear to have been the most significant, as an auction notice of 1855 shows it for sale as part of an estate that included seven public houses and a number of dwelling houses. The brewery earlier appears in

---

4.   See Chapter 1.

Pigot's 1840 Directory for Sussex, where it is listed as being located in Ropewalk,[5] presumably linked to the Albion Commercial Inn.

The East Street site of the Rye Castle Museum is known to be a former bottling plant, although there has been misinformed speculation as to which brewery it served. The fact that the building physically links to the former Blackboy & Still (101 High Street)[6] has resulted in suggestions that the two sites accommodated a brewery of some importance. Certainly, the pub name suggests brewing activity, but the reality is that this concern was not large enough to produce anything more than it needed for its own customers (as did many ale and beer-houses). However, the pub itself was sold to the Chapman brothers (who used it as an off licence) in 1900 and contemporaneous documents show that the brothers also undertook distribution and storage activity from here. It thus seems likely that it was during this time that the East Street site was used for the purpose in question. Some 20 years later, the off licence was sold on to Finn's and it again seems likely that bottling activity would have continued under their ownership.

In the 16th and 17th centuries, prior to any real centralization of the brewing process, many individuals would produce their own beer and sell it to their neighbours. Rye was certainly no different from any other town in this respect, but it is recorded that in 1609 four brewers were fined for supplying beer to unlicensed houses – and that two of these brewers were town magistrates!

The East Street site of the former bottling plant, photographed in 2014

---

5. The same source also shows an adjacent brickmakers' and lime burners', fronted by a member of the same family.
6. See narrative for the Dial House.

Pubs

Albion, Commercial Inn, Ropewalk

There is something of a mystery attached to the Albion. It seems to have started life as a beerhouse, first appearing in town records of 1839 – yet soon after was part of a sizeable brewing empire (attached to a brewery of the same name; see above). After being sold in 1855 it continued operating until closure in 1860.

Baileys, Strand Quay, Rye TN31 7DB.

Rye has had a number of transient food bars which have dabbled in the sale of alcohol, but few of these have offered discrete facilities for the drinker. An exception was Baileys, a wine bar and restaurant that took over one of the old net shop buildings on the Strand (and which had previously been in use as one of Rye's many antique shops). Baileys opened in 2011, had links with the nearby River Haven Hotel and specialised in the mixing of cocktails; but, unusually for a wine bar, it also offered a good selection of beers. Despite some apparent success and popularity, it lasted only until 2014. The premises are now in use by a café and restaurant business (The Old Grain Store).

Although the business has changed, the building has not: the Old Grain Store, 2015

Bedford Arms, 91 Fishmarket Road, Rye TN31 7LR

The first reference to the site on which the Bedford Arms now stands is 1835, when William Apps – part of a well-known Rye family – took out a lease on a piece of waste ground. It is likely that the first building was part of a row of cottages, but conversion to a public house must have happened soon after as, in 1848, George Dann – previously landlord of the Barley Mow – took over the lease and, by 1850, is shown as the pub's second licensee. By this time it was under the ownership of James Batchelor, proprietor of the Landgate Brewery.

The Bedford Arms, 2013

Almost from inception through to the mid-20th century, the Bedford became one of a select number of Rye pubs "adopted" annually by the hop pickers in the months of September and October. Reports of rowdy and sometimes violent behaviour (not unusual in such situations, where tensions could run high) were common.

Sold at auction in December 1923 by Leney, the pub leasehold realised a respectable £1,000. The Bedford subsequently features in numerous accounts of WWII activity, and was chosen as a site for one of the council's air-raid shelters, of the type known as "fly shelters". When landlord Leslie Blackman was called up to the army, his wife Daisy took over its running, and the Bedford Arms become unofficial headquarters for the local Home Guard. At the end of the war, the Rye Home Guard morphed into the *'A' Company Home Guard Old Comrades Association* and continued its association with the pub. In 1943 a convoy, which included a large number of heavy Churchill tanks, caused damage to a kerbstone outside the pub and this damage remained visible for many years.

A 1966 poster for the Bedford unusually advertised iced lagers and also snacks and pies. But it also invited customers to bring a picnic to enjoy on the lawn!

Borough Arms (Blue/Blew Anchor; London Trader), Strand Quay, Rye TN31 7DB

This has had a number of incarnations and earliest records show it as the Blew Anchor (subsequently Blue Anchor) in 1592. It was rebuilt on the same site (upon part of the old town wall) in 1720 and shortly after, in 1728, it became the London Trader, the new name reflect-

Borough Arms

ing a type of ship operating from the south coast ports to London. Like many businesses, the London Trader struggled during the economic downturn in the 1890s, although the landlord showed initiative by trying to diversify and set up a fruit and veg stall in his bar. Unfortunately, his efforts were not applauded by the local magistrates – who fined him for contravening Sunday trading laws. The London Trader was popular, and used as a meeting place by many local societies. In 1897 came a further name change, to the Borough Arms. This name reflected the location of the building (part of the remains of the Borough of Rye's former Strandgate is incorporated within its walls). After a succession of different landlords, the new powers afforded to the police gave them the opportunity to close the pub in 1906. In addition to the usual reasons of falling demand and redundancy, the police also cited rather tenuous safety concerns, relating to the fact that a drunk patron had fallen down the steps. Yet this incident had occurred many years before! There is more than a suggestion that a police officer may have had a vested interest in the Ship, one of its competitors. Following closure, the building failed to sell at auction, and fell into disrepair. Subsequently, however, it was turned into residential property with part later becoming a customs office. In the 1920s, in response to the loss of jobs resulting from falling demand for shipping, the customs house was converted to a Ministry of Labour office.

Architecturally, the place has not changed dramatically over the last century. The original tap room (later the public bar) now houses the Mermaid Corner Tea Rooms and the main building has become a guest house with nine rooms. It has also acquired the prefix "Old". Scenes from the film *The Monuments Men* (starring George Clooney, John Goodman, Cate Blanchett, Bill Murray and Hugh Bonneville) were shot outside the Old Borough Arms in May 2013 (and the tearooms were redecorated as a German butcher's shop in the film).

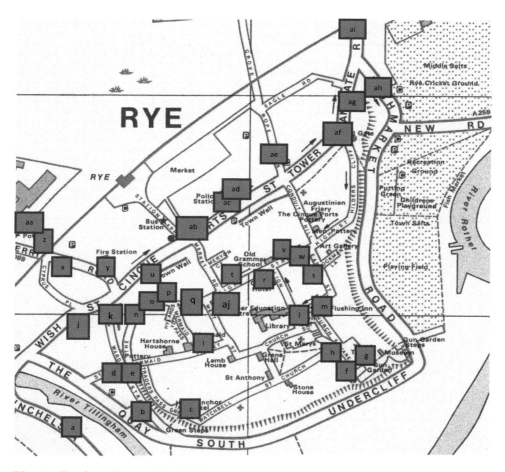

Key to Rye's pubs and hostelries

a - Smeaton Stores
b - Ship Inn
c - Hope Anchor Hotel
d - Bailey's
e - Borough Arms
f - Dolphin Inn
g - Ypres Castle Inn
h - Jolly Sailor
i - Mermaid Inn
j - Greyhound Inn
k - Pipemakers' Arms
l - Red Lyon
m - Flushing Inn

n - Foresters' Arms
o - Swan Inn
p - Standard Inn
q - Old Bell
r - George Hotel
s - Union Inn
t - Whyte Vine Hotel
u - King's Arms
v - Dial House
w - Oak Inn
x - London Stout House
y - Crown Inn
z - Queen Adelaide

aa - Ferry Boat Inn
ab - Cinque Ports / Railway / H&G
ac - Cinque Ports Inn
ad - Cinque Ports Arms
ae - Albion (Inn & Brewery)
af - Tower Inn
ag - Queens Head Inn
ah - Bedford Arms
ai - (to north) King's Head
aj - Le Crowne

Map of Rye © Philip's; Reproduced by permission of Ordnance Survey on behalf of HMSO. © Crown copyright 100043101. All rights reserved.)

Bull/Bull's Head, Longer Street (High Street)

We cannot say with any certainty whereabouts on the High Street this pub was located, but it would appear to have been on the south side. Certainly in existence in 1634, when later mentioned in official records (in 1690) it was attached to a brew house. It started off as the Bull Head (a Catholic Church reference) but common usage resulted in the name changing to the Bull's Head.

By 1735, documents show the Bull's Head to have been an alehouse rather than inn but it was clearly of substantial size, as it hosted a Session Dinner in 1738. It also boasted a yard, garden and stables. It disappeared in 1756, when the landlord moved to the George Inn.

Cinque Ports Arms, Cinque Ports Street, Rye TN31 7AN

Although it was built in 1817, L. A. Vidler[7] advises that this probably opened as an inn in 1820 (although Bagley suggests that it could have been as late as 1838). Very popular in its day, initially incorporating a post house and excise office and offering post chaise hire, it also hosted many society dinners. Before the turn of the century, it expanded twice and later accommodated a new assembly room. The Cinque Ports Arms was another victim of the 1942 bombing raids. Although not completely destroyed (unlike the Cinque Ports Inn – see below) it was severely damaged and did not re-open. Owners Style & Winch sold the property to East Sussex County Council in October 1959, who had identified this as a suitable site for the town's sub-divisional police HQ. However, this does not share the exact "footprint" of the original Cinque Ports Arms.

The Police HQ on the site of the Cinque Ports Arms

---

7. *A New History of Rye.*

Cinque Ports Inn (Cinque Ports Hotel & Assembly Rooms), Cinque Ports Street, Rye TN31 7AN

It is rather confusing that there have been no less than three Rye establishments which have gone by this name (with slight variations), and that the two adjacent ones both incorporated assembly rooms. This version was on the opposite corner of Regent Square to the Cinque Ports Arms and, starting life as a coaching inn built in the early 19th century, became the meeting place for several sports clubs and the Rifle Volunteers. The adjoining assembly rooms were built in 1868, but included within the fabric of the inn, which from this time was known as the Cinque Ports Hotel and Assembly Rooms. The Assembly Rooms had already previously staged pantomimes and plays (notwithstanding that the landlord had been fined for not having a valid theatre licence), but, in 1913, they were greatly modified to accommodate the new and exciting technological development of the day – film screenings. Whilst still an intrinsic part of the pub, the Assembly Rooms then became known as the Bijou Theatre. As such, it remained a highly popular venue for various forms of entertainment until 1931 and showcased many stars, including Ellen Terry.[8] By the outbreak of WWII, the theatre had been sold off and was operating as a separate cinema. But in September 1942, both inn and theatre were bombed and destroyed. Whilst the cinema was rebuilt and reopened, sadly the inn didn't see life again. The cinema itself closed in 1973 and, after standing empty for a number of years, was demolished. The current Regent Motel (at number 42) stands on a part of the Cinque Ports Inn site.

Cinque Ports/Railway/Horse & Groom, Cinque Ports Street, Rye TN31 7AN

The third of Rye's Cinque Ports establishments started life as the Horse & Groom. It probably opened in the early 1830s, but was fully licensed by 1838.

Some commentators have deduced – based largely on its dates – that this was a beerhouse, but it was a very sizeable concern (with at least 15 rooms), which would suggest otherwise. New life was breathed into it by the opening of both cattle market and railway in the town, and in 1869 it changed its name to the rather grandiose Horse & Groom, Railway and Commercial Inn. This was presumably too much of a mouthful, and from 1925 it was known just as The Railway. In 1885 the building was knocked down and completely rebuilt in the form recognisable today. During its demolition, the licence was temporarily transferred to a cottage at the rear. At the end of the 1960s, it underwent its final name change, becoming the Cinque Ports Inn.

---

8. Ellen Terry, one of the leading Shakespeare actresses of her day, had a cottage at Smallhythe Place near Tenterden. This, and the adjoining theatre building, are now owned by the National Trust and are open to the public.

The Horse & Groom at the end of the 19th century

The Cinque Ports in 2014

Crown Inn, Ferry Road, Rye TN31 7DJ

It is generally agreed that this pub started life as the Crown & Sceptre in 1839, although there are claims that it may have opened as early as 1835. Very popular with the seafaring fraternity and fishermen, by the 1870s it had become known colloquially as the "Sailors' House". Smugglers inevitably featured amongst its clientele, and the pub incorporated a tub hole for the storage of contraband.

The Crown, 2014

One of its early landlords was Isaac Wright, who used his pub as a base for other activities and ran a successful horse carriage business prior to the coming of the railway. Rather than allow this subsequent competition to destroy his livelihood, however, he responded by becoming an agent for the LB&SCR.

One of the main attractions of the Crown was for long its ownership of a huge area of land behind, known as the Crown Meadow. This land (long since sold off for development) was much in demand for use by circuses and travelling fairs, and for club days. Despite sometimes attracting police attention, the Crown Meadow was often the focal point for town activities, and much used by the Crown's clientele for the sport of quoits.

During WWII, the Crown promoted the *Dig for Victory* campaign, and the Rye Garden & Allotments Society made their base here. The building was listed in 1972 and, incorporating a night club, now caters to a younger element.

Dial/Dial House, 101 High Street, Rye TN31 7JN

The first reference to this establishment (on the site of what is now the Rye Age UK shop) was in 1820, as the Blackboy & Still. Whilst many pubs with *Blackboy* in the title have links to the slave trade, this does not mean that Rye was so involved: the name was also sometimes used to depict the dark-skinned Charles II. The building was formerly owned by a family of clock makers, and had an interesting and prominent example of the trade at its front, which led to its subsequent change of name. One of its early owners was Stephen Fryman, who was made bankrupt in 1849. This incident understandably made him bitter and, 25 years later, when back on his feet, he bought back the pub. Whether he was determined to make a point or once more failed to make ends meet is open to conjecture, but the pub appears to have permanently stopped trading very soon after, between 1875 and 1878. It was subsequently acquired by Chapman Brothers for use as an off licence, before being sold on to Finn's in the same capacity.

Dolphin, Gun Garden, Rye

A sign for the Dolphin stood in the shadow of Ypres Tower, but records do not identify exactly where the pub itself was sited. In existence by 1710, it closed in 1801 and was demolished in 1837. The name probably reflects that of a ship berthed in Rye Harbour beneath.

It is interesting that Vidler refers to an alehouse of the same name in East Street – opposite Battery House (now the museum). But the dates are similar to those of the Gun Garden Dolphin and, given their proximity, it is tempting to assume that he may have been confusing the two. In addition to the other known Dolphin (which became the Foresters, in the Mint), Bagley refers to yet another, in the High Street, between 1715 and 1773. Whilst it would not have been unusual for a maritime town such as Rye to have more than two establishments sharing the same name (particularly with maritime connections), this remains something of a puzzle.

Ferry Boat Inn (New Inn), 67 Ferry Road, Rye TN31 7DJ

More than one of Rye's alehouses bore this name, or variations on it, in the 18th century, although none of the others were as enduring. First mentioned in 1709, the Ferry Boat Inn probably took its name from a ferry service running to Cadborough. The pub passed through many different hands before being bought by the East Guldeford Brewery in 1866. After a protracted battle with the licensing authorities, the pub was completely rebuilt and re-opened in 1899. To mark this event, its name was changed to the New Inn.[9] From its re-opening to the end of WWI, this was one of the most popular and successful pubs in the town. But it increasingly struggled through the 20th century. In the 1960s it reverted to its former name, and its disappearance soon after

---

9. The New Inn was a very popular pub name of the period, but the magistrates (whilst granting the change of licence), lamented the pub's loss of its former identity and links to the past.

from local records suggests that it may have closed for a few years. From the mid-1970s it is again listed in directories, but closed for good in 1991. It is now a private residence.

Flushing Inn, Market Street (Butchery), Rye TN31 7LA

The original building, standing at the corner of the former Pump Street[10] and Market Street, was of 13th century origin, but destroyed in the wake of the fire that followed the 1377 French raid. However, the barrel-vaulted Norman cellar survived and remains to this day.

The present building dates from the early 16th century and first became a hostelry in 1729. The owner then was John Breads[11] – a butcher by trade – who maintained a slaughter-house in the backyard. It was in 1743 that Breads was found guilty of Rye's infamous "murder in the churchyard", when he allegedly attempted to murder the mayor James Lamb. There is still controversy over what exactly happened that night, but Breads killed the wrong man; ignorant of this fact, he allegedly ran through Rye proclaiming that "butchers should kill lambs!" What cannot be disputed is the fact that Breads was convicted of murder and sentenced to hang; and that on his last journey, to the gallows, he was allowed the request of a final drink – in his own pub!

The origin of the pub name is also something that is open to question. Rye had strong smuggling links to the continent and it may be that the Flushing Inn reflected the Dutch port of Vlissingen. The inn itself was certainly heavily involved in smuggling. Equally plausible is that the name was a corruption of "fleshers" – the old English name for butchers (particularly as, in addition to Breads's profession, the inn was situated in the Butchery).

In 1850, the building became subdivided into three separate properties, although much later – in 1994 – it reverted to its original state. In 1905, renovations uncovered a 16th century fresco (wall painting), which was restored and subsequently prominently displayed. Visitors queued to see this and, even in 1936, were still prepared to pay 3d (1p) for the privilege.

Throughout its long life, the status of the Flushing Inn has undergone change. For a period it was unlicensed and has even oper-

The former Flushing Inn, 2013

10. Now part of Church Square.
11. Sometimes spelled "Breeds".

ated as a private club. By 1960, the Flushing had become a hotel and restaurant. Despite having traded profitably for many years, it closed in 2010 and now – as it started life – is in private use.

Foresters Arms (Dolphin), 44 The Mint, Rye TN31 7EN

This pub first traded as the Dolphin around 1826. Offering accommodation of varying levels it enjoyed early, but not lasting, success.

In 1865, it changed its name to the Foresters Arms and became effectively a common lodging house. Increasingly struggling with the competition (the Swan and the Standard) on its doorstep, when the landlord lost his licence for permitting drunkenness on his premises in 1895, the writing was on the wall.

Although continuing under a new landlord, it is no surprise that the Foresters Arms closed just two years after the 1904 Licensing Act came into force. However, as with the Borough Arms, the landlord may have felt that he was being victimised, as he had only shortly before been fined for allowing drunkenness on his premises. In this particular case a potential customer had turned up drunk and been refused service; but the police successfully argued that, in walking from the front door to the bar, he had been on the premises. Rough justice, indeed!

The former Foresters' Arms, 2013

George Inn/Hotel, 98 High Street, Rye TN31 7JT

The George has for years been one of the premier and iconic inns of Rye, and heavily involved in civic life. A George Hotel existed as early as 1575, but was then situated on the Butchery (Market Street), opposite the Town Hall, moving to its current site in 1719.

Now opposite the historic old grammar school, the square windows and columns do suggest an 18th-century construction. However, if these features are undeniably Georgian, they reflect a reconstruction: some of the wall and ceiling beams identify that the original building was in fact Tudor. The fine balcony has been widely used by speakers on a multitude of occasions and is still utilised on civic occasions, particularly when the newly elected mayor drops heated pennies to the children congregating below (a custom only interrupted by WWII).

Conspiracy theorists might conclude that the authorities had it in for the George as, in 1650 (when in the Butchery), the landlord was fined for having an oversized sign – which spilled over onto Corporation land. This was a pretty unusual case to say the least but, by a strange quirk of fate (or not?), the hotel was prosecuted for the same offence in 1812 when in its new location! Six years later, Lewis Meryon added the fine assembly room, with music gallery and bow windows, which proved very popular with farmers coming into town for the Saturday corn market and which was also used to hold dances and concerts.

One advantage that the George held over its rival the Mermaid was that it stood on one of the wider streets of Rye and could thus operate as a coaching inn. In the days of the coaching service between Rye and London, the George served as the terminus and hosted the famous *Diligence* coach, which made its celebrated last journey from here in 1845. Shortly after, the inn's chandeliers were lit for the first time, when the Lord Mayor of London opened the newly built railway at Rye in 1850.

Less celebrated was the George's heavy involvement in the murky activity of cock fighting. In more recent times, it has sometimes struggled to successfully balance its dual roles of hotel and classy drinking establishment. The hotel is clearly its bread-and-butter business and unfortunately the bar is not particularly large. This is not too much of a problem in the winter months, but can cause difficulties at peak holiday times. Accordingly, in 2011 the management

The George Hotel, 2013

declared that drinks would only be served to those dining there. This was perceived by local drinkers to be a move to exclude them and a boycott was instigated. As is often the case, after acrimonious exchanges in the local paper, the issue was resolved; but the incident serves to demonstrate just how seriously people of Rye take the matter of where they drink.

George Tap, Lion Street, Rye TN31 7JT

Standing on the corner of Lion Street and the High Street, the George Tap was effectively the public bar of the George. For most of its life it was a simple beerhouse operating separately (under its own licence), but at some point in the 1870s it became a fully integrated part of the hotel.

Globe Inn (Globe Spice / Globe Marsh), Military Road, Rye TN31 7NX

This attractive, weather-boarded building has been a public house since 1834, and was known as the Globe by 1839 (if not before). Bagley suggests that this may at one time have been known as the Ypres Globe Inn, but there is little to corroborate this. For most of its life it has traded simply as the Globe, although the suffix "Spice" was added in 2013, and changed to "Marsh" in 2014. It is the only commercial property in Military Road and, although predating all the listed buildings in the Military Road conservation area, it is the only one unlisted.

In its early days, the Globe was well patronised by navvies working on Royal Military Canal improvement works. There was at one time an underground tunnel from the Globe leading to the canal, which has since been walled up by the council, for safety reasons. It seems very unlikely that this tunnel would have been constructed for any purpose other than smuggling;

The Globe, with adjacent forge, 1930s

it is also highly probable that stories of the place being haunted by a lady in white were concocted by the smugglers to keep outsiders away!

At some point, the pub acquired the adjacent forge and blacksmiths (Suttons forge), which is now used as its car park.

The history and ownership of the pub reflect many local names and traditions. The lease was assigned to East Guldeford brewer Herbert Verall Chapman in 1883 and later came under both the Courage & Barclay and Style & Winch banners. And in common with many Marsh pubs, there is a history of longevity in terms of management, with the Ames family behind the bar between 1859 and 1903. This gives the Globe the distinction of having been the longest family-run pub in Rye. It also had the honour of being the headquarters of the Military Road Bonfire Society at the turn of the 20th century, and for a few years in the 21st century did service as an Indian restaurant.

The Globe and beer garden, pictured in 2013 (top). Some quite obvious changes were made in 2014 (below, right), although local opposition to the threat to the beer garden remained – as demonstrated by posters in a house opposite the pub (below, left)

It is unusual for a pub of this size to have boasted such a large beer garden – it was almost a quarter of an acre in size and very popular in the summer months. In its time it also hosted an excellent skittle facility. In March 2013, however, its existence came under threat when a planning application was made to construct two three-bedroom houses on the site. There is almost nothing like change to a popular local pub to unite the community, and this resulted in 300 people signing a petition opposed to the move. Rye Town Council duly rejected the proposal, although this may also have owed something to the risk of landslips: the garden suffered from such in both the late 1990s and in 2000. However, following an appeal to the Planning Inspectorate, permission was obtained in August 2014 and construction of the new houses commenced in early 2015.

The pub had a very well publicised overhaul in 2014, coinciding with another change of management. The re-vamped and rustic interior has been described as "visually busy", with indoor clapboard and corrugated iron walls. The unisex toilet is also very innovative for a town like Rye!

Greyhound Inn, Wish Street, Rye TN31 7DH

The Greyhound was another of the beerhouses that appeared following the 1830 Act. First references to it appear in 1838 and 1839, although an earlier – unnamed – beerhouse may have existed on the same site. It closed in 1863 when the landlord was declared bankrupt, only to re-open the following year. The Greyhound closed perma-nently in 1906, another of the early victims of the 1904 legislation. It was sub-sequently converted into two cottages before being demolished and replaced by two semi-detached houses.

The Greyhound circa 1895 and housing on the same site in 2014

Hope Anchor/Hope & Anchor, Watchbell Street, Rye TN31 7HA

Parts of this building date to the 15th century. It is not listed as a beer retailer/beerhouse until 1838, but very soon after applied for and received a full licence. Up until 1870 its taproom was separately licensed, a situation contrived to make full use of the 1830 Beer Act.[12] It was reputed to be a rough pub, frequented mainly by fishermen and sailors and, after numerous scrapes with the law, it closed in 1864 – only to re-open soon after. Used as a lodging house by labourers it remained less than genteel, although its customers were not without redeeming qualities. This was illustrated by an unfortunate event which occurred in 1881 when the landlord's son attempted to commit suicide by cutting his own throat. This was a well reported and discussed incident, with blood sprayed all over the bar. But the regulars gathered round, staunched the flow of blood and, hailing a passing doctor, managed to ensure that his life was saved.

The Hope & Anchor subsequently passed through the hands of a number of local brewers (including James Body of Brighton, also a noted wrestler of his day) in quick succession before being purchased by Bowens in 1890. Although its reputation improved as a result, it nevertheless bumbled along with no great success or patronage until WWI, when it closed. In 1925 the building was enlarged (more or less to its current form) and re-opened – promoting itself with what was almost certainly the first vegetarian menu in the town. At this time it also changed its name from the Hope & Anchor to the Hope Anchor. It is a source of debate amongst historians why there should be so many pubs that display these slight name variations, but the Hope Anchor is a more accurate representation of the name given by mariners to a vessel's "spare" anchor.

The Hope Anchor suffered some minor damage in WWII, but it is hard today to reconcile this fine hotel (which dominates the entrance to Rye from the west) with the den of iniquity that preceded it.

The Hope Anchor enjoys an enviable cliff-top location (2013)

12. Although not common, such an arrangement was also utilised by Rye's George Hotel.

Jolly Sailor, Church Square, Watchbell Street, Rye TN31 7HE

On the south side of Church Square, the Jolly Sailor was another of the beerhouses that sprung up in response to the 1830 Act, and it wasted little time in applying for a full licence. This was granted in 1832 at the second time of asking. It seems that the initial reluctance of the magistrates was fully justified, as this was to become arguably the roughest of Rye's rough pubs and was very regularly visited by the police.

Some commentators have described it as being only a shade above the workhouse, and it became a refuge for many who would otherwise have slept on the streets. Its landlords were reluctant to turn away any trade, and overcrowding was a regular concern – it is said that upwards of 30 would be accommodated at any one time, many of whom would sleep slumped against a rope. An occasional lodger was the itinerant owner of a dancing bear, which was chained to a heavy post and locked in a shed at the rear of the building. The 1904 Licensing Act was designed with such establishments in mind and, indeed, the Jolly Sailor became a victim of this legislation, although surviving until the end of 1910. Its name lives on, however, in one of the Hope Anchor's bedrooms.

This building, pictured in 2013, is the former Jolly Sailor. Its advertised credentials – "Good Accommodation for Travellers" – can still just be seen on the brickwork (at the top)

King's Arms (William IV), 11 Cinque Ports Street, Rye TN31 7AD

This pub started life as a beerhouse on the site of what is now Cinque Ports Antiques, yet another consequence of the 1830 Act. Opening sometime between 1830 and 1840 under the name of the William IV, it changed its name to the King's Arms in either 1866 or 1867. For much of its life it had a seedy reputation, with drunkenness and prostitution rife, and one of its landlords was imprisoned for tax evasion. Towards the end of the 19th century it arguably improved, although could still be "lively" when the hoppers were in town. Given the number of other pubs in the vicinity, it is no surprise that it, too, was on the police "hit list" and after an unsuccessful attempt to close it in 1906, it finally lost its licence in 1909. It was demolished a few years later.

The site of the former King's Arms, 2014

Kings Head (Top o' the Hill), Rye Hill, Rye Road TN31 7NH

Partly because it was then situated outside the Rye parish boundary (the boundary was changed in 1935), records for the King's Head are not as extensive as for other Rye pubs. Some sources identify it as a 17th century building, which may have first served as a coaching inn – and its position would support this stance. By the late 18th century it was certainly

A packed car park (seemingly hosting a car rally) at the Top o' the Hill, 1990

The Top o' the Hill in January 2014, prior to being re-signed and reopening

operating as a pub, being a centre for the very unpleasant practice of bull baiting. There is also documentation suggesting that it was already quite established when used for billeting 200 soldiers here during the Napoleonic Wars.

Newspaper reports of the 19th century show it was a popular and thriving concern, although one article records a robbery taking place here on Christmas Eve in 1870. It also accommodated numerous coroners' courts and inquests. In the 1980s, the pub changed its name to the Top o'the Hill, reflecting its geographic location.

Under new management, it was sold in the summer of 2013 and after extensive refurbishment reopened in 2014 under its former name.

London Stout House (Huggett's Beer House/Two Sawyers), 32 Ferry Road, Rye TN31 7DN

This tiny property started life in the mid-19th century under the name of Huggett's Beer House. By the 1870s it was known as the Two Sawyers[13] – reflecting the occupation of the landlord and his son. The fact that it additionally acted as a cheap lodging house and, like the Jolly Sailor, accommodated not only the owners of dancing bears, but also their charges (whose antics would keep neighbours awake at night) in a yard at the back gives a good indication of the nature of the pub. Later it was taken over by the Chapman Brothers and, in 1892, after a landlord was charged with drunkenness, they tried to change its image. As part of this process, it was renamed the London Stout House, reflecting the Coombe's London Stout House product that Chapman's was promoting. But this presumably cut little ice with the authorities, who used the 1904 legislation to close the pub in 1908. It is sited almost opposite the Crown and remains a distinctive building.

---

13. And sometimes by locals as The Sawyers Arms or simply just The Sawyers.

London Stout House 2014

Mermaid Inn, Mermaid Street (formerly Middle Street), Rye TN31 7EY

This lovely inn with its Georgian façade has several claims to fame, but few would deny that it really is one of England's loveliest inns. Even though it has not continuously held a licence, it is certainly one of the oldest inns in the country, although there is debate as to how far back parts of the current building date. Evidence suggests that an original Mermaid may have been built in 1156, the same year that Rye was admitted to membership of the Cinque Ports. Little detail is known, however, and it is by no means certain that it then stood on the current site. More detailed records show that, in 1300, there was a Mermaid Inn in the present location, constructed of wattle, daub, lathe and plaster. It also boasted a cellar hewn from rock. At this time it charged a penny a night for lodging and guests could drink beer brewed on the premises. However, the particularly aggressive French raiding party in 1377 razed it to the ground. At least the cellars – with their barrel-vaulted ceilings – survived and a new building was constructed over them. This project spared no expense, utilising baulks of Sussex oak and ship's timbers and fireplaces carved from French stone. The new construction was built to last and, indeed, the basic structure has remained substantially unaltered down the years.

In 1530, the Mermaid harboured Catholic priests fleeing the continent in the wake of reformation and between 1550 and 1570 – reflecting its growing prosperity – it was used by the Town Corporation for celebrations, including those of Mayoring day. It is claimed that Queen Elizabeth may have stayed there in 1573 (although it is more likely that she slept at the Customs House – then known as Grene Hall). The French Ambassador certainly stayed at the

The beautiful and historic Mermaid Inn (photo: courtesy Judith Blincow)

Mermaid in 1654 and it has long been popular with the literary and thespian set. Ellen Terry, Hilaire Belloc, Rupert Brooke, Ford Maddox Ford, A. C. and E. F. Benson, Rupert Brooke and Henry James have all been amongst its patrons.

The Mermaid has had some well-documented links with smuggling over the years, and one of its bedrooms – *Dr Syn's Bedchamber* – contains a bookcase that doubles as an emergency exit, confirming its slightly murky past. The Hawkhurst Gang were patrons in the mid-1750s and, when drinking at the Mermaid, its members would brazenly display their pistols on their table. Such was their fearsome reputation that few magistrates dared to interfere with them. One of their number was Thomas More who, having finally been arrested and bailed, stormed into the Mermaid and grabbed the bailiff who had informed on him. The poor bailiff was taken to the harbour and was about to be thrown into the waters below when the captain of the revenue sloop intervened.

Probably because of its reputation as a safe house for smugglers, the Mermaid was rarely used for civic functions after 1750. As the forces of law and order began to win their battle with smuggling, the fortunes of the Mermaid declined and, following a major fire in 1888, it reopened in 1895 as a private hotel. After another change of ownership in 1913, it was run as a private club and subsequent attempts to regain a full licence fell for many years on stony ground, given the strong temperance movement in Rye. It was not until 1945 that, when the Mermaid was again being run as a hotel, a full licence was granted. Owing to mounting debts it closed again in 1949, only to reopen once more shortly after.

The building itself, as well as its wonderful setting, now draws visitors from all over the world and it is widely acknowledged to be the hotel of choice for the discerning visitor. Other notable guests have included Charlie Chaplin, Richard Burton, Harry Secombe, Prince Edward, Warren Beatty, Kenneth More, Ken Russell, Pierce Brosnan, Robert Vaughan and Johnny Depp. And, in 1982, the hotel hosted a private luncheon party for HM the Queen Mother to mark her installation as Lord Warden of the Cinque Ports.

The age and history of the Mermaid dictate that there are a multitude of claimed ghosts. There is a roll call of at least ten hauntings, which includes two grey ladies and another who makes impressions on a bed. The most preposterous are a full pitched battle and a pair of duellists, complete with doublet and hose, crossing swords; one decapitates the other and throws the body down a secret trapdoor! Presumably this haunting only occurs very late at night after a very long session at the bar!

Oak Inn/Pig & Whistle, 106 High Street, Rye TN31 7JE

Sited between Broad's candle factory and Broad's warehouse, this beerhouse came into being soon after the 1830 Act and started life as the Pig & Whistle.

Favoured by local fishermen, it changed its name to the Oak in 1881 and proved to be one of the more enduring of Rye's beerhouses, lasting until 1909. It, too, was a victim of the 1904 Act, although, curiously, owners Style & Winch failed to attend the arranged hearing. It subsequently became a tea-room, but is now occupied by an art gallery.

The former Oak Inn (2014)

(Ye) Olde Bell Inn, 33 High Street, Rye TN31 7EN

The Bell is a pretty Grade II listed building with a small but attractive courtyard garden. It is one of a number of inns to lay claim to the title "oldest in Rye" and is probably the oldest continuously fully-licensed premises in the town. Some sources suggest it was established in 1520, but there are reliable grounds for believing that it may have been built fully a century earlier. It is claimed that the beam above the public bar was part of the original building – and that the beam itself was formed from a tree growing on the spot where the pub stands. The name may commemorate the reclamation of Rye's own church bells, stolen in a French raid but recovered in a retaliatory attack.

The interior of the Bell (top; late 1960s) and exterior (2013)

As with the Mermaid, it is claimed that Queen Elizabeth once visited.[14] More verifiable is that the Bell was involved with smuggling, with tunnels beneath – one of which connects to the Mermaid – and that it too was patronised by members of the Hawkhurst Gang in the 1730s and 1740s. It further boasted a revolving door system to enable (contraband) goods to be delivered anonymously.

---

14. There is no suggestion that Queen Elizabeth was an habitué of Rye! There is evidence of only one visit by the Virgin Queen, and it seems that many establishments vied to maintain their status in the town by claiming her as a patron.

An arguably lesser but commonly heard claim to fame is that the Bell has been frequented by local residents the Cheeky Girls!

Olde Worlde Wines, 56 Cinque Ports Street, Rye TN31 7AN

A relative newcomer on the scene, Olde Worlde Wines opened in 2010 and since then has offered the drinkers of Rye an experience somewhat different from the norm. Essentially a wine shop or off licence specialising in wine, this unpretentious building also operates as a very cosy, homely and atmospheric wine bar, with wooden floor and soft furnishings. The place is lit by candles and, at weekends, it offers customers the chance to visit and taste in the (also candlelit) cellars.

Olde Worlde Wines

Pipemakers' Arms (Ye Olde Pipemakers' Arms), Wish Street, Rye TN31 7DH

Standing on the corner of Wish Street and Wish Ward, the Pipemakers' started life as a beer-house in 1830 (although probably not then known by this name). It was popular with workers at the adjoining net factory, many of whom were housed in three-storeyed houses immediately behind the pub. Stories are told of drunken net workers being ejected from the pub – straight into the arms of Salvationists playing outside.

The pub underwent significant alteration in 1907 and has changed considerably in size and shape since Edwardian times. When sold at auction by Leney & Co in December 1923, it raised the sum of £2000 (more than any other Rye pub). In common with the Bedford Arms, it had a fly shelter installed at the start of WWII. Later in the conflict, it survived (relatively unscathed) a bomb that destroyed two cottages next door. In 1966, it changed its name to the more pretentious Ye Olde Pipemakers' Arms. This was short-lived, and it reverted to its original name six years later.

The Pipemakers' Arms in 1900 (left). The building and its setting were far more pleasing on the eye than in 2013 (right)

Queen Adelaide, 23 Ferry Road, Rye TN31 7DJ

Given Rye's standing as the jewel in the crown of Sussex, it is rather surprising to find such an excellent example of a Kentish half weather-tiled 18th century building as the Queen Adelaide.

Sited close to the railway (on the Udimore side), the building initially comprised three separate cottages. The original beerhouse was opened around 1832 by the Albion Brewery, occupying the middle cottage. The subsequent expansion resulted in two entrances and three bars, each of which was on a different level, with the lowest – the games room – being accessed via steps. It was not until the 1980s, however, that the partitions were fully removed.

The Queen Adelaide c1950 (left) and in use as an internet café / brasserie in 2014

In the 19th century, the pub earned a reputation (supported by magistrate and police reports) for being a hang-out for the rougher elements of society, and later became one of the town's pubs that were patronised by visiting hop-pickers.

In July 2006, the pub was the victim of a fire that was attributed to a local arsonist. Two fire crews tackled the blaze but extensive damage was caused to the ground floor, with further smoke damage to the first floor. Whilst it re-opened, it closed again in 2008. The writing was on the wall when purchased by Tesco, who had designs to demolish it to create road access for a proposed development (notwithstanding that the land behind the pub earmarked for development was owned by Sainsbury!). It did again briefly reopen in 2011, surviving into the following year. It is currently operating as an internet café cum brasserie and, although the supermarket development has now been abandoned, the prospects of the Queen Adelaide serving again as a traditional pub are surely very slim.

Queens Head (Two Brewers), 19 Landgate, Rye TN31 7LH

This was part of a tenement of six cottages, built around 1575. It became the Two Brewers from (probably) 1706,[15] although the first recorded licence was issued in 1722. In 1796, the property was divided into two, with one of the buildings becoming the Queens Head. The Queens Head is thus significantly smaller than its predecessor. At one time, the building had a Georgian appearance, but the corbelled canopies and eaves date from a change of landlord in

The Queen's Head (early 2014)

15. Bagley advises that there were references in records of both 1655 and 1656, but it has not proved possible to verify this.

the 1880s. In the 1900s it became quite a stronghold for goal running, being headquarters for the town team. After struggling in the early part of the 21st century, the Queens Head underwent a revival following the staging of regular folk and blues music and a commitment to the provision of real ale. Its accommodation bears names that reflect the title of the pub, including the Elizabeth, Boadicea and Mathilda Rooms. In 2014, it incorporated a more unusual venture: a summer Saturday barbeque enterprise run by two former soldiers under the name *And the Kangaroo Said*. This offered such exotic fayre as alpaca, crocodile, camel, zebra and, of course, kangaroo meat.

In September 2014 the council gave outline planning permission for conversion of the Queens Head to cottages, a holiday let and commercial premises, but it was still trading in October 2016.

Red Lyon/Red Lion, Lion Street, Rye TN31 7LB

Whilst the Mermaid and George were always the chief inns of the town, the Red Lion was in its day demonstrably the next in line in terms of status. Although much smaller than the other two (at no time offering more than four rooms for accommodation), it developed a very good reputation and hosted many of Rye's major civic events.

As with many other establishments, its early history is open to debate and there is a choice of historians offering variations on a theme. 1574 has been quoted as the date of inception, but David Russell has offered evidence of a pub or ale house on the site in the 1550s. Although, sadly, there are no surviving plans showing the Red Lion in its entirety, we know that it was a two-storey building with two acres of land, which included a yard used for mail and passenger coaches.

There are well-documented accounts of the history of the Red Lion from 1709 onwards. In addition to frequenting the Mermaid and the Bell, members of the notorious Hawkhust Gang

Simon the Pieman Tea Rooms. Within these rooms is arguably the only physical reminder of the once-influential Red Lion (2014)

were regular patrons in the 18th century, and between 1735 and 1785 all the town's Sessions dinners were held here. The Red Lion was heavily implicated in the treating scandal of 1852, which resulted in the then mayor of Rye, Jeremiah Smith (whose other claim to fame was being the country's largest hop grower), being imprisoned for giving perjured evidence. The candidate Alexander McKinnon had hosted an extravagant meal at the George Inn, costing the princely sum of £230, but the bill had been settled by a third party, advanced by Smith; and McKinnon subsequently left the £230 under a sofa cushion in the Red Lion.

Unfortunately, the Red Lion was destroyed by fire in 1872. The fire took hold in the main bar and the largely wooden structure was engulfed. Nothing could be done to save it, but the tireless work of the fire brigade and many local residents (aided by a rainy night) did at least manage to prevent the spread of the fire to neighbouring properties. The Red Lion was not rebuilt and a new Board school opened on the larger part of the site two years later. The only salvageable part of the building is today occupied by the Simon the Pieman Tea Rooms, which contains what is claimed to be the original 16th century inn fireplace. At least the name of the street in which the Red Lion stood commemorates its part in local history.

Ship Inn (Cock & Coney/Duke of Wellington), The Strand, Rye TN31 7DB

Whilst many pubs in the area were involved in the smuggling trade, the Ship's role did not conform to the norm. Built in 1592, it initially served as a warehouse for the storage of contraband seized from smugglers. From time to time, the authorities would auction the goods and before long a small bar was established so that potential buyers could sample the wares. Bagley suggests that it did not become a pub until 1836, but this is not the complete picture. Whilst it is true that it did not obtain a full licence until then, by 1722 it was trading under a limited licence, as the Cock and Coney.[16] In the 1820s it became the Duke of Wellington and took on the current name when the licence changed in the 1830s.

Sited amongst the distinctive old warehouses now given over to antique and other shops, the Ship is a sizeable pub, which retains a beamed bar and authentic panelling. Another Rye pub that was popular with the disenfranchised, at one time it boasted a number of separate

The Ship pictured in 2013. In recognition of its original use, a board on one of the outside walls records the names of vessels involved in efforts to combat smuggling

---

16. "Coney" being a term for rabbit.

bars and has for a long time offered accommodation. It was damaged in a German air raid in 1939; and three workmen repairing the roof were killed in a follow-up raid shortly after (although the pub suffered no further damage). The pub name painted onto the outside of the building unusually uses lettering of Egyptian lineage.

The Standard Inn, The Mint, Rye TN31 7EN

Dating in part from 1420, the building was originally constructed as two properties, which later merged, and it is thought to have been first opened as an alehouse around 1600. Just how long it served in this capacity is open to conjecture, as records show it as opening anew around 1860, at around the same time as its neighbour, the Swan.

The local magistrates – with the backing of temperance groups – made it clear that they were not keen on three pubs in such a small area, and the Standard took on a new lease of life from 1906, when both the Swan and its other neighbour – the Foresters Arms – became victims of the 1904 Licensing Act. It then became home to a number of town clubs and societies.

This attractive pub, with beams, exposed brickwork, open fire and courtyard was highly popular in the 1980s and 1990s, but suffered a downtown after the millennium. This resulted in its closure in 2013, but it re-opened under local management as a boutique hotel (but retaining a pub on the ground floor) in 2014. The extensive renovation exposed the original 15th century carved beams and brickwork, which have been retained as a striking feature.

The Standard in 2013 and the adjoining Swan Cottage Tea Rooms, formerly a pub in its own right

Swan, 41 The Mint, Rye TN31 7EN

The history of the Swan mirrors that of its next door neighbour, the Standard, being built in the 15th century and enjoying an indeterminate period as an alehouse before re-opening in the mid-1860s. It differed in that it always seemed to be much quieter than its neighbour. So much so that the Swan voluntarily offered to surrender its licence under the 1904 Act – the only pub in Rye to do so. The Swan thus closed in 1906, although this does not tell the complete picture. The landlord had made a deal with Edwin Finn: the brewer wanted the property as a bottle store and the magistrates were happy to exchange the licence, with the former landlord becoming the store manager.

The name lives on, in the building's current guise as the Swan Cottage Tea Rooms (see photo of the Standard).

Tower Inn, Landgate, Rye TN31 7LH

Established in the 1840s, the Tower Inn was sited between the former Two Brewers (present Queens Head) and the Landgate itself. It closed in 1910, the victim of the aforementioned rather unsatisfactory legislation that allowed police and magistrates very arbitrary powers of closure. In this case, the magistrate stressed that there were no concerns as to the manner in which the landlord had conducted himself or his business; his only crime was to be situated close to two other similar establishments (the Queens Head and Bedford Arms) which were deemed to fully satisfy the local need.

The Tower Inn, c. 1870, and the premises in current use (2014)

Union Inn, 8 East Street, Rye TN31 7JY

Some internet sites (presumably replicating the same source) describe the Union as an old mediaeval building serving as a pub since 1420. This is baffling, as reliable sources identify it as a 16th century cottage which became a beerhouse in the 1830s and subsequently expanded by taking over its two neighbours. The painting on the outside wall (of a rose, thistle and shamrock) was only revealed after redecoration work in the late 20th century. It has been restored, although nobody is sure of its provenance; but it is clear confirmation that the pub name commemorates the 17th century Union of the Crowns. What is puzzling, however, is the lack of a daffodil in the depiction (of the home countries, Wales is not represented).

Given its age, it would be surprising if the Union had no claim to ghostly activity and, indeed, it purports to be the most haunted of all Rye's hostelries. During renovation work, the bones of a young girl were found secreted within a wall. Whilst this is horrific to us today, it was not unusual for unbaptised babies (particularly those who died in childbirth) to be entombed in this way; however, this girl was past infanthood and the discovery has been put forward to explain some of the many "sightings". The Union's roll call of ghosts also includes: an unknown seafarer; an unmarried mother who fell to her death down the cellar steps; and a seventeen-year-old girl walking through the kitchen (although how anyone can pin down her age so precisely is a further mystery!). In 1994, paranormal researchers who were trying to ascertain the source of a rather unpleasant smell pervading the building claimed that they witnessed doors opening and shutting by themselves. As someone who used this pub at the time, to this author's untrained nose the smell had little to do with the spirit world and everything to do with drains!

Closed in 2013, this is another of Rye's pubs to have reopened in 2014, although it is now more a steak house than traditional pub.

The Union Inn, 2014

White Vine (Vyne) Hotel/White Vine House, 24 High Street, Rye TN31 7JF

Built between 1560 and 1570, the White Vyne (as it was originally named) was constructed over a mediaeval cellar. One of the earlier buildings on the site was almost certainly destroyed in the same French raid that accounted for the Mermaid and devastated the rest of the town. The lounge and Elizabethan dining rooms were renovated in 2005, but retain some of the original oak panelling. The White Vine has served as both hotel (with bar) and private residence over its lifetime. At one time residence of Rye mayor Pix Meryon and later the family of historian and writer William Holloway, from 2011 it became home to the Ambrette Restaurant – a "restaurant with rooms" and wine bar (pictured in 2014). Now trading again as a hotel and restaurant under its own name (the Ambrette has moved to another part of town[17]), it claims to be haunted by the ghost of (yet another) white lady, and – more imaginatively – poltergeists, which inhabit the kitchen and one of the bedrooms. The former mixes up fresh vegetables, whilst the latter delights in flinging pillow cases around the room!

The White Vine Hotel

Ypres Castle Inn Rye, Gun Garden Steps, Rye TN31 7HH

Parts of this attractive weather-boarded building standing in the shadow of Ypres Tower date back to 1640, with significant subsequent development taking place in the Victorian era. One Rye historian has described it as "being up and down the steps from time immemorial", and another as "a noble relic of times long gone by, casting its halo o'er the past of Rye", although records of it operating as a pub date back only to the 1830s.

---

17. Following a dispute with the landlord, the Ambrette moved out to new premises (also in the High Street) in early 2015.

The picturesque Ypres Castl, 2012

Commanding fine views over the Romney Marsh and of the River Rother and conveniently sited next to the Gun Garden, the Ypres has traditionally been frequented by the fishing fraternity, and at one time fish was sold from one of its bars. Its location near the river meant that its cellar was sometimes the first port of call for smuggled contraband landed in the town. The inn sign remains as depicted by Whitbread in its 1949 series of miniatures, one of the few pubs that can make such a claim.[18] In recent times it has had a boules piste, although this was sacrificed when strengthening work to the cliff was required to prevent the garden falling into the road below. It has also been known to transform one of its rooms into a sushi bar for the duration of Rye's scallop festival. The Ypres even has its own stocks, a deterrent to poorly behaved children.

Other pubs/alehouses/beerhouses

Rye has hosted numerous other drinking establishments about which much less is known. Perversely, this is not because records are poor, but rather that the many histories of Rye provide clues that are not present in those histories of other communities. Many towns of similar size have only sketchy records predating the 19th century and their apparent paucity of pubs or alehouses is often a reflection of a lack of knowledge.

Those additional Rye drinking establishments of which we know and which are no longer with us include:

---

18. The Whitbread logo has been removed, however, to reflect its current status.

- **Barley Mow**, Landgate – press reports of 1839 and 1840 suggest that this held some significance but other than that only landlord records (confirming existence between 1832 – 1845) can be found.
- **Chequer(s),** Market Street (The Butchery) – referred to in a document of 1671.
- **Clarke's Beer House**, The Mint – recorded in 1864.
- **Dolphin**, High Street – recorded by L. A. Vidler between 1715 and 1773, but little else about this is known (see also entry for Dolphin, Gun Garden).
- **Ferry House** (location unknown) – mentioned in a document of fines of 1722, the source (as well as its date) makes it clear that this is a different establishment from the Ferry Boat Inn in the above narrative. Also different from both is a further **Ferry Boat Inn**, referenced in 1735.
- **Fortune** (location unknown) – recorded as operating from 1754, but possibly predating this time. Closed in 1758.
- **Hoy** (location unknown) – recorded in 1739 and 1757, but closed by 1758. The name is an old English word for island.
- **King's Arms** (location unknown) – this is referenced in 1722 and would appear to be different from the Kings Arms in Cinque Ports Street (which appears on the scene later on).
- **Lamb**, Landgate – different sources suggest that this opened in either 1835 or 1838 and closed in 1845 or 1847. Clearly, it had only a short shelf-life.
- **(Le) Crowne** (corner of West Street and High Street) – there is a record of Lord D'acre staying here on his way to meet Henry VIII at Calais in 1520. It appears to have closed in 1562.
- **Maypole** (location unknown) – fleeting mentions in archives of 1707 and 1709 show that there was an establishment of this name somewhere in the town.
- **Morphotes Tippling House**, Strand – precise location and dates unknown.
- **Ports' Arms** (location unknown) – referred to in a document of 1722 (ref. Geoffrey Bagley).
- **Prince of Orange** (location unknown) – referred to in a document of 1707 (Bagley).
- **Queens Arms**, Middle Street, 7–9 West Street – referenced in documents of 1655, 1656 and 1722.
- **Red Cross** (location unknown) – referred to in document of 1722 (Bagley).
- **Royal Oak**, Hilders Cliff (precise location unknown) – believed to be an alehouse in the 17th century.
- **Rye Gally** (*sic*), Tower Street – Bagley states that this pub (probably an alehouse) operated from 1757 to 1780. Vidler also includes it in his list of six inns serving the town in 1772. Whilst other sources confirm the date of closure, licensing records suggest that it was operating earlier, by 1739.
- **Shipp (Without)** Landgate – recorded as operating between 1720s and 1745.
- **Ship In Distress** – recorded between 1709 and 1752, and sources suggest that it was sited in Tower Street. Vidler, however, produces some persuasive evidence that it was nearby in Cinque Ports Street, close to the waterworks.

- **Sims Beer House**, The Strand – there is just the one reference to this, in 1883, where George Sims is identified as the owner.
- **Swan**, The Butchery – identified by David Russell as trading in 1581.
- **Three Kings**, Middle Street (Mermaid Street) – Russell has identified references in both 1576 and 1590.
- **Three Mariners**, 15 High Street – Russell has identified reference to an alewife residing here in 1592.
- **White Swan** (location unknown) – mentioned in connection with the infamous treating scandal of 1852. It is possible that this is the Swan in The Mint (although this is unlikely as other records do not show the Swan as trading at this time)

Also of interest is a Whitbread pub sign that stands outside a house on the A259 at the western entrance to the town. This bears the name "Smeaton Stores", commemorating the engineer James Smeaton, who designed an ill-fated harbour at nearby Winchelsea Beach (amongst other more impressive feats). There is no evidence that the property ever served as a pub, but it was an off licence for many years, and was one of the properties sold at auction by Leney & Co in December 1923 – fetching an impressive £850.

6

Other Marsh Towns: Lydd and New Romney

Lydd

Pigot's Directory of 1840 described Lydd as "a place of no thoroughfare". For centuries it had been an island, but Pigot's reference is to the fact that the town – the most southerly in Kent – was not really on the road to anywhere significant, and was more likely to be a destination than part of a route. This has now changed, with the growth of coastal communities, the power stations and the RSPB bird reserve at Dungeness, and the development (and proposed expansion) of its own airport.

Lydd was formerly a port of substance and corporate member of the Cinque Ports, as a *limb* of New Romney; but it has a number of other claims to fame, including the magnificent "Cathedral of the Marsh", and has hosted a highly significant army presence over the last century. The town's development has been mostly reactive, in response to the coming of the railway, the army occupation and the staffing needs of the nearby power stations. Although the railway may give the appearance of still running, it's only so by courtesy of sporadic exchanges of nuclear fuel flasks (no more than once a week). The army – which once had a specialist flying corps based at the Rype (Lydd's huge green) – put the town on the map with its development of Lyddite explosive, but now has a reduced role, and the power stations also operate on much lower staffing levels. Its army presence meant that Lydd was targeted during WWII and suffered numerous bombing raids, which inflicted meaningful damage – including the destruction of one of its pubs.

As established in Chapter 1, Lydd has also been home to two breweries. Finn's High Street operation was certainly the more impressive, and all its residents became accustomed to the sound of the brewery hooter, which blew at 6.00 am for the start of work; again at 8:40 am to signal breakfast; at noon for lunch; at 1.00 pm for return to work; and at 6.00 pm (finishing time). It may be a cliché, but it really was the case that local residents set their watches by the Finn's hooter. Finn's brewery at one time employed nearly 30 staff, which included three coopers, and also set up a canteen within the Lydd camp, where beer would be sold to the troops.

There is now no obvious sign of the Rising Sun brewery established by Thomas Haisell, although the names of two adjacent properties in New Street – Sunrise Cottage and Sunset Cottage – offer a tangible clue to the location. The brewing operation was sited behind the

Ladson Lodge (left) and Sunrise Cottage (foreground) with Sunset Cottage behind, in 2014. The brewery was to the rear

pub, between the cottages and Queens Road, where garages now stand. There have been suggestions that, at times, some limited brewing may have taken place at Sunset Cottage and/or at Ladson Lodge, but this is difficult to verify. Ladson Lodge, in Ness Road, is connected to Sunrise Cottage and the three properties form an "L" shaped footprint. It is not known exactly when the brewery buildings were demolished, although a 1925 sale document relating to the pub refers to a "ginger beer factory used by the Lydd Brewery".

In contrast, up until 2015 there was still much to be seen of the former High Street brewery, as developed by Edwin Finn. This site was over an acre in size, and Finn had ensured that the buildings were built to last. After brewing had stopped, the site was purchased in 1946 at auction by another well-known Lydd family business – Blacklocks[1] – which used the premises for their Lyddite Chicks hatchery[2]. This subsequently became famous throughout Europe. Whilst Blacklocks constructed some new poultry sheds, they retained most of the buildings, modifying them simply by adding ventilation. Unfortunately, the iconic brewery tower – which as a landmark was second only to the church tower and had seen war service as a luxurious lookout and communications centre for the network of local airfields – was demolished shortly before the hatchery was sold (to Grampian) in 1970. Soon after, the site and buildings were acquired by Servo Ltd. The original office, bottling plant, garage and stables (converted to housing) could still be identified up until the summer of 2015.

1. At the time, the Blacklocks family were also the proprietors of the general stores at Prospect Corner (and the family also appears within the history of the George Hotel).
2. Ironically, the hatchery had started out behind the Rising Sun and moved to the new High Street site in 1948, some two years after it had been purchased.

Key to Lydd's pubs & breweries

a - Army camp canteen
b - Royal Oak
c - Red Lion
d - Royal Mail
e - George Hotel
f - Dolphin Inn
g - former New Inn
h - Finn Brewery site
i - (likely) site of Three Mariners' Inn
j - former Beehive Inn
k - former Rising Sun (and brewery site)
l - site of First & Last
m - Star Inn
n - former Bridge Inn (Station Hotel)

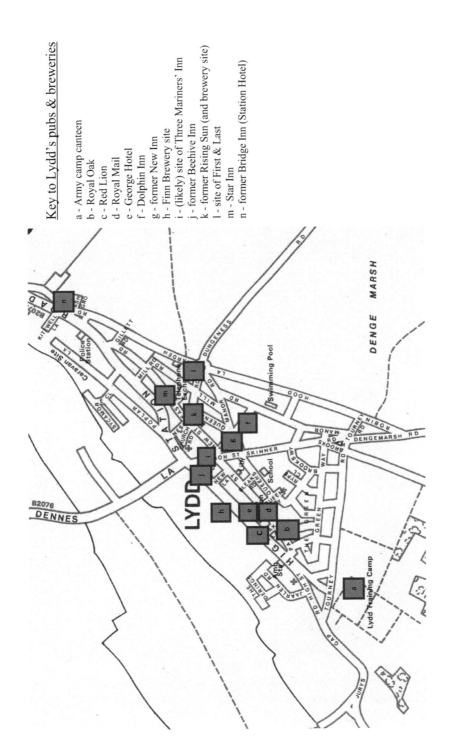

The site of the former Finn's Brewery seen from the two entrances from the High Street (one adjacent to the former Beehive pub; the other one opposite the George) in March 2014. The old Lyddite Chicks hatching sheds were still clearly evident from the Vinelands estates at this time (bottom)

View of Finn's site (centre) from Lydd church tower, 2014

For long viewed as a prime housing location, it was safety concerns over the limited access to the site that precluded it being developed and, although planning permission was granted in 2011, this was allowed to lapse. However, with formalities at last completed, work commenced in 2015. Inevitably, most of the former buildings have been demolished, but it is pleasing to see that the fine exterior of the Brew House has been afforded listed status and this remains. The names of some of the new houses also reflect the heritage, and their address is now, fittingly, Brewers Close.

Given the roles of the army, railway and power stations, it would be reasonable to expect that many pubs have come and gone over the years in Lydd; surprisingly, however, detailed records show only around a dozen having existed in any substantial form in the town.[3] Claims have been made that the early 19th century building at No. 1 High Street was also once a pub; but, apart from a hanging sign bearing the name of "Galleon", there is no physical evidence to support this, and directory records list it only as a post office, newsagent and tobacconist, bookseller, and tea rooms. Similarly, there is no record of the current Chinese takeaway at the end of Ness Road ever serving as a pub, despite the hanging sign bracket. There is one histor-ical reference to a pub or beerhouse named The Mariners, but this is slightly ambiguous and may or may not relate to the Three Mariners. As befits a military town, a number of Lydd's

---

3. *Bagshaws 1947 Directory* does list beerhouses maintained by William Ditton, William Lawrence and William Prebble, although no addresses are provided. Given that the entries for Lydd extended further afield, it is likely that at least two of these were on the shingle close to Dungeness (as covered within Chapter 2).

pubs – notably the Beehive – have attracted a certain reputation for violence at various times. In addition to the one pub destroyed in WWII, there was also a celebrated wartime incident in another, which put the town firmly on the map. Even the keenest drinker might question whether hanging is justified for ordering the wrong tipple, but this was arguably behind the incident that brought the Rising Sun to national attention (see below).

Another wartime story concerns an acute shortage of beer. Pubs within the town were swamped by troops, many of whom preferred the conviviality of local hostelries to drinking within camp. But it was a failure to plan ahead properly, rather than any problem caused by rationing, that brought matters to a head in 1944 when the harvest was being gathered. Those involved in the harvest have always worked long hours and have traditionally slaked their thirst into the small hours; and the demands made by them and the local soldiers meant that the pumps ran dry. The situation that arose was well encapsulated by Councillor A.J. Pope who wrote: "We are lucky if the pubs can open two nights a week. There was more beer in 1940. It's a disgrace!"

Beehive Inn, 6 & 8 High Street, Lydd TN29 9AJ

The first recorded reference to the Bee Hive (as it was initially known) is in 1715, although it may have closed before being re-established as a beerhouse in the 1830s. It is shown as such within a sale document of 1857, well before it became Finn's brewery tap.

Although no longer licensed, the old Beehive Inn still stands, well preserved and bearing its former name, next to the butcher's shop. It is now two separate dwellings, and the former entrance to the second bar (at the western end) has now been filled in. References to it are nearly always prefaced by "notorious" or "infamous". Although there have been a number of pubs in Lydd that have been classed as "rough", resulting in no small part from the army

The Beehive in 2013

presence, the reputation of the Beehive seemingly owed much to the practice of hosting both cockfighting and prizefighting. Where each is concerned, the activities continued long after they had been outlawed.

Bridge Inn (formerly Railway Hotel), 129 Station Road, Lydd TN29 9LL

The rise and fall of the Bridge Inn mirrors the fortunes of the railway, which was its *raison d'etre*. One of three railway hotels[4] on the Romney Marsh, this was built with almost indecent haste. Land was leased from the Council and plans promptly approved so as to allow its completion (in 1882) only a year after the New Romney Branch line opened.

The renaming of the inn may appear inconsequential, but the reality is that the adjacent bridge is something of a curiosity on the Marsh. It is in fact the only overbridge on the railway line. Ironically, when the road became utilised by heavy power station traffic, it was deemed inadequate to cope, necessitating the building of the road diversion and level crossing in front of it (although most vehicular traffic continues to use the bridge). Local historians still argue as to whether the cost of this crossing was met by the railway or the power station.

The decline of the railway wasn't quite the death knell for the inn, but it struggled thereafter, despite becoming a free house. For a time (in the 1980s) it operated a towing caravan park in its grounds. The last licensee, despite being severely disabled and needing to keep both zimmer frame and medical supplies behind the bar, struggled valiantly to keep the inn open. However, on his death in 2010, the Bridge closed. The current dishevelled state suggests that its only future lies with change of use.

The Railway Hotel, c1900 (left); and the faded glory of the Bridge Inn in 2013 (right)

---

4.   The others being at New Romney and Appledore. Only the one at Appledore has served passenger trains in recent years (but see separate entry in Chapter 3).

Dolphin Inn, 11 South Street, Lydd TN29 9DQ

The Dolphin, whose name reflects Lydd's maritime past, occupies the site of an earlier inn, which was allegedly once owned by Thomas à Beckett, 12th century Archbishop of Canterbury. The current timber framed two-storied building purportedly dates from 1764 and is interesting in its own right, with barely a straight wall to be seen. A newspaper reference to an auction being held here in 1769 would suggest that it may have always served as a pub. The building was afforded Grade II listed status in 1973.

During World War II, the Dolphin's yard housed what was colloquially known as "the gas chamber". This is not as sinister as it may seem: it was essentially a caravan filled with smoke that was used for training in and testing the use of gas masks. Photographs at and around this time show an additional brick wall at the Rype end of the building, which housed the gents' toilets. More recently (in the 21st century), the car park hosted Lydd Best Kebab before the latter moved into more suitable and permanent accommodation within the High Street.

This popular back-street local is the closest of Lydd's pubs to the Rype and it is thus not surprising that it has been home to numerous sports clubs. But, in addition to fielding football, cricket, darts, cribbage and pool and teams, it was also a major venue for hare coursing (and has laid claim to hosting the John Jones Coursing Club). It was here, too, that bat and trap, once a popular activity on the Marsh, was re-introduced in 1949 by new landlord Bill Baines, who had arrived from a pub in Canterbury – a real stronghold of the game. There are also stories of a resident ghost. After closure for a short time in 2014, the Dolphin opened its doors again in 2015.

The Dolphin, pictured in 1980, has changed little in recent years

First and Last, Ness Road (SE end, adjoining roundabout), Lydd TN29 9EL

It is not known when the First and Last opened for business, but it is another of the pubs that first appears within local directories of 1871. Its demise, however, on 29 August 1944, was rather more widely reported. On this day, a doodlebug hit by ack ack fire exploded on top of a barn at Granary Corner (where the Youth Club now stands). In addition to the barn, three other properties were demolished, including the First and Last. The photograph from the 1930s (left; courtesy Ted Carpenter) shows it to have been a substantial property and, post-war, a bungalow and two houses were constructed on the site.

The site of the former First and Last, pictured in 2013

George Hotel, 11 High Street, Lydd TN29 9AJ

This imposing 1620 Grade II listed hotel – built on the site of an earlier tavern – is steeped in history and tradition. It has been used to hold prisoners prior to trial and been a staging post for London coaches. Inevitably, however, it has featured most prominently within smuggling lore. Indeed, the so-called Battle of Lydd in 1721 took place near the George, after smugglers Jacob Walter and Thomas Biggs had been taken as they came ashore at Dungeness. They were manacled, brought to the George and placed under armed guard. The following is an eyewitness account by landlord Stanton Blacklocks:

> They was in a chamber, 6 officers with them, 20 firelocks loaded with powder and ball. at 5 o'clock on Sunday night 9 men well mounted and as well armed with pistols, swords, coopers adzes, wood bills and forks, comes up to ye house, dismounts from their horses and runs upstairs, firing all ye way. They wounded 3 officers and got between the officers and their arms and carried away Walter and Biggs; if these 9 men had not carried them off, a 100 more was hard by ready to make another attack. Jacob Walter was later recaptured by a commander in the Queens' Dragoons. The outcome of Thomas Biggs is unknown.

Being one of the most prestigious buildings in the area and sited next to the Guildhall, the George has hosted ceremonial events, including annual meetings of the Commissioners of the Levels. Of architectural note are an unusual double door arrangement that gives access to the town hall and a Priest's Hole (which may in reality have been built more as a hiding place for contraband). Of numerous claimed George ghosts, the most cited haunting is of one of the bedrooms, which allegedly hosts either the spirit of a young lady entertained by the old mayor or a suicidal smuggler.

The George pictured at the end of the 19th century

Another function inevitably afforded the George was the staging of coroner's courts and inquests. The records of these often make for interesting reading and in this respect the George is no exception. In addition to deaths that can be attributed to involvement in the free trade, a particularly sad event stands out from 1883. This was the demise of a young child who was burnt to death when, wandering too close to the hearth, his nightshirt caught fire. The boy's mother was at a neighbour's house at the time, and the jury considered that there had been neglect on her part.

Unfortunately, the George no longer holds the same status as formerly, and in recent years has struggled to meet its sizeable overheads. In March 2013, owned – as several other struggling concerns such as the Seahorse (Greatstone) and the Plough (New Romney) – by Enterprise Inns, the landlord declared himself bankrupt. After closing for just a few days, the George was taken on by another local. But the underlying problems could not be masked and at the end of the year it closed again. It has once more re-opened but its long-term future must be subject to conjecture, although plans to develop Lydd Airport may offer it a lifeline.

The front and rear views of the George, 2012/13

New Inn, 7 South Street, Lydd TN29 9DQ

First references to the New Inn appear in 1839, which strongly suggest that it may have been one of those beerhouses to have emerged following the 1830 Beerhouse Act. It was still

The former New Inn premises are now occupied by a dental practice (2013)

trading during WWII, when it was pressed into service to cook meals for troops based in the town (soldiers had been billeted in houses vacated when the locals were evacuated, as Lydd camp was heavily targeted by German bombers). Trade never really picked up after the war, although it limped on into the next decade, closing in the mid-1950s.

Queen of Bohemia

The existence of the Queen of Bohemia has only very recently come to light, by dint of diligent research undertaken by Romney Marsh historian and Lydd resident Ted Carpenter. Although there is no indication of its location within the town, the Commissioners' and Expenditors' report of 1669–83 reveals that civic meetings were held there as well as at the George, suggesting that it had some prominence. The name would have been a tribute to James I's daughter Elizabeth Stuart, whose husband, Frederick V Elector Palatine, became King of Bohemia in 1619.

Red Lion(?) 42–48 High Street TN29 9AN (St Nicholas House)

Like the Queen of Bohemia, the Red Lion has not been recorded in any other histories and has only been identified through the research of a former resident and the current incumbent of St Nicholas House, the Right Reverend Damien Mead.

St Nicholas House c. 2010 (photo courtesy Roy Hipkiss)

As can be inferred from the numbering, this has not always been one building, although it is unclear when sub-division first took place. The building itself is fascinating but the number of inglenook fireplaces would argue against the original use being as artisans' cottages, as is sometimes suggested. The date above what is now the main door shows 1693, although this probably denotes the time when the property was altered and the current window recesses installed. The rear of the building has been dated to 1598, but the foundations – of oak frame and stone – have been estimated as being laid around 1420. Documents and indentures for numbers 42–44 suggest that it was in use as an inn prior to the establishment of the George further up the High Street; and, although not fully legible, these further suggest that the trading name may have been the Red Lion. This would have been prior to 1620 (when the George opened), but the rest is open to conjecture. It does seem that its existence was short lived, but a reference in the aforementioned documents to stabling, the foundations of which were subsequently discovered during renovations, imply that it had some prominence within the town.

A recent discovery has been the existence of what was once a concealed room, accessed from floorboards above. Its location means that it is unlikely to have been a priest's hole and its size (sufficient to accommodate 6–7 people – or vast quantities of smuggled contraband) also lends weight to the notion of the Red Lion having been a sizeable concern.

Rising Sun, 34 & 36 New Street, Lydd TN29 9DJ

The earliest confirmed reference to the Rising Sun is in connection with the attached brewery in 1832, although it is likely that that it was trading by 1800. The pub was quite large by the standards of the day, and it is possible that some brewing activity was also conducted here at various times, as discussed earlier.

There has been some confusion as to the specific purpose served by each of the current buildings over the years, which is understandable given their ages. The properties now known as Sunrise and Sunset Cottages did, indeed, comprise the Rising Sun pub. These sit on the corner of New Street, at the junction with Ness Road; but Sunrise Cottage does also adjoin the property in Ness Road known as Ladson Lodge. Observers will note that the roofline suggests that the original conjoined buildings were actually Ladson Lodge and part of Sunrise Cottage – and this is the case. The original building was constructed around 1600, and the extension added about 50 years later. This work was independent of the brewery buildings.

During the 20th century, it was in the Sunrise Cottage part of the property where the main drinking took place. This had no cellar, so barrels were stored in what is now Sunset Cottage and rolled into the main bar when required. Sunset Cottage later also hosted the saloon bar. There have been suggestions that drinks may have been served from (a part of) Ladson Lodge at some time, although this would seem unlikely. Another claim has been made concerning Ladson Lodge: that it was once a coaching inn. Lydd, of course, had a coaching inn in

The Rising Sun, c. 1960 (left; photo courtesy Ted Carpenter); and the same building in 2013 (right)

the Royal Mail, although there are records of coaching inns existing up to 100 years before the Royal Mail was built. So, although again unlikely, this possibility can't be discounted in its entirety.

By all accounts, the Rising Sun was a very popular pub. It had some colourful landlords, one of whom – when caught in a compromising situation with a barmaid – jumped out of the bedroom window rather than face the wrath of his wife, breaking his leg on the pavement below! Another, who had just closed the pub for the night, found a drunk local trying to access his safe, and chased him down the road with a shotgun.

But it was another incident that put the pub firmly on the national map. At nine o'clock one October morning in 1940, landlady Mabel Cole was on cleaning duties. She was surprised when a stranger with an unfamiliar accent came in and ordered a cider champagne. There were two things that contributed to her surprise: it was illegal at the time to order or serve drinks before 10 am; and cider champagne had long been discontinued, although an old poster which was displayed outside the pub advertised its charms. Given the general paranoia at the time – when even sporting a beard could result in the wearer being reported as a potential spy – Mabel called the police. For once, suspicions were fully justified: the stranger turned out to be Karl Heinrich Meier, a Dutchman of German origin who had landed at Dungeness along with three accomplices a few hours earlier. A few weeks later Meier, together with two of his colleagues, was hanged at Pentonville Prison.

There are local stories told of "foxing" (the snaring and shooting of foxes) expeditions to Dungeness, which were very popular during and shortly after WWII and which would commonly start with the collection of beer from the Rising Sun. It has never been satisfactorily explained why the fox population at Dungeness was so high at this time, but there are records of over 80 foxes being shot in a day on the 'Ness. Expeditions from Lydd were highly popular and would be all-day affairs; and there are reports of parties returning to the Rising Sun with a "pot" of 15–20 animals.

The Rising Sun remained in the Cole family until well after the war. The family additionally ran a butcher's shop in the same road, and advertising in the 1950s and early 1960s urged customers to pop into the pub on the way back from purchasing their meat! Numerous regulars reported seeing the ghost of a young woman in the pub, who would sometimes disappear through the wall adjoining Ladson Lodge. This is believed to have been that of a Ladson Lodge employee, who was jilted at the altar. The pub also served as the headquarters of the local RAOB (Royal Antediluvian Order of Buffalos), before closing in the early 1980s.

Royal Mail, Park Street, Lydd TN29 9AY

What is now a very comfortable back-street "local" additionally providing accommodation, was once a major part of Lydd life. It was built in 1746 as a coaching inn, to cope with the increasing volume of coaching traffic. In 1925 it was owned by George Beer & Ringdens of Maidstone, which gave it the distinction of being the only pub in Lydd not owned by Finn's. In the 1990s and early 2000s, it was quite a community pub, fielding teams in various local sports and quiz leagues. It was a group of Royal Mail regulars who were instrumental in creating Lydd's "Pirate Friday" in 2006, which started out as a very local affair centred on the pub, but which now involves all Lydd's hostelries.

The Royal Mail in 1920 (left) and (little changed) in 2013 (right)

Royal Oak, Park Street, Lydd TN29 9AX

The Royal Oak was originally two cottages joined together, and was subsequently extended. It is difficult to establish exactly when it opened as a pub, although Finn's took it on from 1888. It is not listed within *Kelly's Kent Directory of 1882*, so the presumption is that either Finn's were the first to obtain a licence; or that it became a pub in the intervening six year period. After struggling at the end of the 20th century, it closed for a short time before re-opening in November 2000.

The Royal Oak in the early 20th century (left) and 2013 (right)

The Royal Oak featured in some unwelcome publicity in 2012 when a group of five drinkers attending a Halloween fancy dress party there launched an assault on a group of soldiers. One of the soldiers was badly beaten, and the assailants were later each given custodial sentences.

Star Inn, 16 Station Road, Lydd TN29 9EB

This attractive old timber-framed building probably dates from the early 17th century, or even earlier, making it one of the oldest in Lydd. It was listed in the 1871 directory, but almost certainly trading as a pub prior to then. It was part of the Style and Winch stable by the late

The Star in the 1920s (left) and shortly after closure in 2012 (right)

1920s, and still with them in 1956, when the company was taken over by Courage Barclay. Later, its two rooms were knocked together to create a larger single bar. Widely described as being a popular and comfortable locals' pub, it seems to have led a fairly uneventful existence, although the Star did feature in a coroner's court record of 1902. A soldier, experiencing a case of unrequited love, spent an evening in the pub. This may not be an unusual occurrence in a military town, but less usual was the fact that the soldier was teetotal, and used his time there to compose a letter. After leaving the pub he threw himself in front of a train; and it transpired that the letter was a suicide note.

Its popularity with generations of locals made the closure of the Star in 2012 all the sadder. Despite rumours of sale and plans being drawn up for refurbishment and re-opening, it alas remains closed at the time of writing and it seems inevitable that, whatever its future, it will not be as a pub.

Three Mariners, High Street, Lydd TN29 9AJ

Ted Carpenter has again been instrumental in identifying a pub of this name from court records of 1818 (some smugglers having been arrested there). The likely location was the building standing at the junction of High Street and Cannon Street. Although there have been suggestions that this building was operating as a pub at the turn of the 20th century, photographs in the early 1900s show it trading as a confectioners prior to it being taken over by National Westminster Bank. The bank has also since closed (in 2008), but the building remains. Coincidentally, it bears an uncanny resemblance to that of another Three Mariners, at Hythe (see Chapter 4).

The building believed to have once been the Three Mariners, pictured in 2014

The Canteen, Military Camp, Lydd

THE FINN-ISHED CENOTAPH

It may seem somewhat incongruous, but one of the most popular places to drink in Lydd around the turn of the 20th century was the Army canteen. This was, of course, largely to do with the number of army personnel stationed in the town, but also testimony to the marketing and popularity of Finn's beer (it was Finn's that set up and ran the establishment). It was to all intents and purposes a pub within the camp, and was established in 1897. Its demise as the result of a fire in September 1919 was described by some as a "tragedy". The event was sufficiently significant to be recorded by camp artist and photographer A.E. Shaw (image, left, from Ted Carpenter collection. This is titled: "The Finn-ished Cenotaph").

The fire does not appear to be the end of the story, however. Assets listed in documents relating to the sale of Finn's estate in 1921 include The Canteen. It is listed as a leasehold beer off-licence and store, so presumably was by then operating under a much different guise. It is not even clear if this was on the same part of the camp.

New Romney

The history of New Romney makes a fascinating tale. The town – now fully a mile and a half inland – was originally a harbour town at the mouth of the River Rother and was one of the original Cinque Ports. As such, it was required to maintain ships ready for the crown in case of need. In return, the town received numerous concessions, most notably freedom from national taxation.

The south coast suffered a series of heavy storms throughout the 13th century, but none was more severe than that that of 1287. In addition to almost destroying the town, this filled the harbour with mud, sand, silt and other debris. Even more significantly, the route of the river was permanently diverted to enter the sea near Rye. Despite the fact that New Romney declined markedly after the loss of its harbour, it still retained civic responsibilities and consequently displays a rich heritage. There remains much to see in New Romney, and in that can be included some of its historic pubs. Outside of these, the town hall and the church of St Nicholas are worthy of special note. The latter was situated close to the harbour and there is still a mooring ring attached to it. Further, the church is one of a number of older buildings having steps leading down from the pavement. This is a tangible reminder of the silt and debris thrown up by the aforementioned storm, which raised the level of the surrounding land.

What is remarkable is that – despite its size and status – New Romney has never been home to a brewery of any significant size. There are hopes that a new venture, the Romney Marsh Brewery, may change this in the fullness of time. Starting life in April 2015, the original venue was intended to be a converted outbuilding in Coast Drive at Lydd-on-sea. However, planning permission was granted for only three years, so the decision was taken to locate in New Romney's Mountfield Industrial Estate instead.

The vision of Matt Calais, a TV producer[5] who had felt the need to escape from London and move down to the Marsh, this is a family-run 12-barrel micro brewery, capable of producing 2,000 litres of beer at a time and up to 5,000 litres a week (bottles and cask). Under the slogan "Hand-reared on the Kent Frontier", the naming of the Romney Marsh Brewery's staple beers (Romney Amber, Romney Golden and Romney Best bitters) reflects their origin.

Despite the lack of brewing heritage, the town – perhaps because of its former status – boasts some of the country's oldest licensing regulations (or maybe more accurately the oldest *recorded* licensing regulations). In 1414, the bailiff and Jurats of the town decreed that "all priests and those who commonly frequent the taverns, should be in their houses where they

Early production days at the Romney Marsh Brewery (photos courtesy Matt Calais)

---

5.   Probably best known for the long-running series *Come Dine With Me.*

ought to pass the night, at 9 o'clock at the outside". This rather intriguing regulation carried a swingeing penalty fine of 6s 8d for non-compliance. In 1427, the annals record that "2 men called ale conners should be chosen to strain and taste the beer made in the town, the makers of the beer to send for the tasters to approve the same, and if good upon proof, they shall sell it for a penny halfpenny and no more, if not good, then at a penny." In 1528, the price had come down, and it was ordered that "all beer is to be sold in Romney at three quarts for a penny – any alewife[6] who infringed this order to be fined 12d and forced to give up her tavern".

Records also suggest that New Romney hosted a great number of pubs and alehouses in the 17th and 18th centuries. Unfortunately, not all these were identified by name and many seem to have disappeared before the 19th century. Those named include **The George**. This – understandably – was located in George Lane and in Elizabethan times accommodated the entourage of the Lord Warden when he visited the town, if the Dolphin was not used. The George was also regularly used to hold court cases. Others identified in local records include the **Queens Head**. It is interesting to note that Sessions Meetings are recorded with members dining "at the *Sign* of the Rose and Crown and sometimes at the *Sign* of the Queens Head". This is a reminder of why early pubs were required to erect signs: because many of the population were illiterate, signs had to convey the name without words and accordingly attracted prominence in local life. Another pub identified in records is the intriguingly named **Golden Bacchus Inn**. Although there is little known about this pub, in the 1700s, it was both highly popular and widely advertised. The latest record of this pub is a newspaper reference of December 1768, notifying that it was to host an auction the following month. As with Lydd, there are a number of beerhouse keepers (in this case three) listed in *Bagshaw's 1847 Directory* who cannot be matched to known pubs.

Inevitably, New Romney played a key part in smuggling activity, and there are still signs of a network of tunnels that linked many of the town's buildings in connection with that purpose.

Blue Dolphins Hotel, Dymchurch Road, New Romney TN28 8BE

Now standing alongside the A259 on the route to Dymchurch, the property known as Blue Dolphins was built in 1507 as a water bailiff's cottage facing the harbour, and flourished under various guises. It had been a coffee house, academy of music and boarding house before becoming the hotel and restaurant it was until very recently. It has also at times been home to a netmaker, tanner, woolstapler, fisherman, vintner and cobbler.

Underneath the property is a blocked door which once gave access to part of the town's network of smugglers' tunnels.

---

6. This confirms that at this time, the keeper of alehouses was usually the woman of the household.

16th CENTURY HOTEL & RESTAURANT

Situated in the historic Cinque Port of New Romney the Blue Dolphins Hotel combines 16th century charm with modern facilities to make it the perfect place for both long and short break holidays. Single, twin and double rooms are available within the hotel and there is also a two bedroom family cottage. The popular candle-lit restaurant, which is open to non-residents, offers excellent food in delightful surroundings.

Room rates, including full English or Continental Breakfast, start from £27.00 per person per night.

DYMCHURCH ROAD, NEW ROMNEY, KENT TN28 8BE
Telephone/Fax: New Romney (01797) 363224

A 1984 advert for the Blue Dolphin (left) and the building in 2014 – now in private use but very little changed (right)

Broadacre Hotel, North Street, New Romney TN28 8DR

The Broadacre Hotel is a charming back-street, ivy-covered Victorian building situated in North Street (which runs parallel to the High Street), and which has a bar open to non-residents. Its location unfortunately means that most travelling through New Romney along the A259 are totally unaware of its existence. It started life as a farmhouse, and the main building (comprising the entrance and six of the nine bedrooms) probably dates back to the 17th century. It has been expanded over the years with the incorporation of an adjacent 1860s cottage (which provides the remaining bedrooms) and an estate agent's office – the single-storey building that now houses the bar. For a time (and well into the 1950s) it was a country club before becoming a hotel and (in 2009) a four-star guest house. At one time it was known as The Gables. It is little known that the Broadacre appears within the 1950s Ealing Comedy *Green Grow the Rushes* (which starred Richard Burton and Honor Blackman). In this film, the Romney Marsh has become Andromeda Marsh, and the hub of the local community is the *Andromeda Arms* (the Broadacre). This film includes some excellent external shots of the building, as well as some fascinating footage of New Romney (and other parts of the Marsh) of the time.

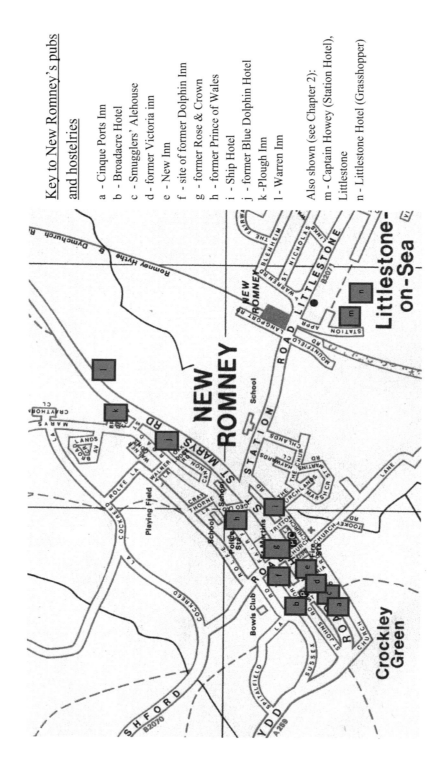

Key to New Romney's pubs
and hostelries

a - Cinque Ports Inn
b - Broadacre Hotel
c - Smugglers' Alehouse
d - former Victoria inn
e - New Inn
f - site of former Dolphin Inn
g - former Rose & Crown
h - former Prince of Wales
i - Ship Hotel
j - former Blue Dolphin Hotel
k - Plough Inn
l - Warren Inn

Also shown (see Chapter 2):
m - Captain Howey (Station Hotel),
Littlestone
n - Littlestone Hotel (Grasshopper)

Cinque Ports Inn, 1 High Street, New Romney Kent TN28 8BU

Claiming to be one of the oldest continuously trading pubs on Romney Marsh, this cosy hostelry with low-pitched roof and low ceilings has been in the same family for generations. It was built in the 18th century, on the foundations of an earlier building, and has changed little over the years. It retains a number of discrete small bar areas and also has a pleasant beer garden. The inn's sign depicts one of the oldest heraldic devices, three 14th century ships each with the head of a lion. The Cinque Ports hit the local news headlines in January 2016 when a motorist crashed into it, causing some spectacular structural damage.

The Dolphin, North Street, New Romney TN28 8DR

It is reported that, in Elizabethan times, the Lord Warden would be entertained at "the sign of the Dolphin", and this was undoubtedly an influential inn of its time. There are rumours that the Dolphin was connected, via the network of underground tunnels, to the Gun House in Cannon Street and the Ship (although there may have been confusion arising from the similarity of its name with that of Blue Dolphins; see above). The inn has long gone, although an ancient wall, the name "Dolphin Spot" and a plaque bearing the picture of a dolphin are tangible reminders of the site's past.

New Inn, 37 High Street, New Romney TN39 9JH

In the same way that there is little new about New Romney, the New Inn – the largest hostelry in the town – was new only in 1381,[7] when originally built (reputedly by monks). Although parts of the original survive, the current façade is obviously Georgian.

Its first proprietor is listed as a Peter Newin – an interesting illustration of the custom of the time of individuals taking surnames from their occupation or trade. For a time, the adjacent building housed the town gaol (complete with dungeon). This was being used increasingly infrequently and in 1750 was bought by, and incorporated into, the inn. By 1785, the New Inn was a scheduled stop on the Rye–Hythe stage; the timetable referred to it as a "genteel" establishment.

The New Inn was once used to hold coroner's inquests and also by civic dignitaries when meetings of the Confederation of the Cinque Ports of Brotherhood and Guestling were held at New Romney. Its age dictates that there are a number of stories attached to it. One such is that, during the 18th century, a young woman called Elizabeth was found hanging from the staircase in the New Inn, and there have been sightings of this mysterious lady walking the hallways and rooms of the inn. A long-blocked up chimney breast also confirms its smuggling involvement.

Appearing in *The Loves of Joanna Godden*, the New Inn has at times been a base for New Romney Cricket and Football Clubs and was until recently a busy town centre pub, offering

The New Inn, pictured just prior to refurbishment in 2013

---

7. The most recent sign stated 1380, although its predecessor showed 1381– the date preferred by most historians.

usual fayre such as a Sunday carvery and live music at weekends. Its previous collection of small intimate rooms was long ago transformed into one bar area. Unfortunately it closed in 2015 and has since reopened as a coffee shop. Planning permission has also been sought to build houses on the car park at the rear.

The Plough Inn, Dymchurch Road, New Romney TN28 8UF

It is not known whether any insider trading was involved here, but the construction of the Plough took place at the time that the country's highways were being improved under the authority of the Turnpike Trust. Very soon after the Plough had been completed (in 1776), the Rye–Dover road was turnpiked here. The front of the Plough was hurriedly redesigned so that travellers could step from the inn to waiting coaches, and vast stabling facilities – catering for 20 horses – added. The whole estate covered 2 acres of land and included hen houses and piggeries.

But even at this time, the Plough did not cater solely to the affluent. In the attic, two stout ropes were strung across the beams and those who had over-imbibed would be draped across them to sleep it off. For obvious reasons, this became known as the "two-penny rope".

The first keeper of the Plough had a licence limited to the sale of ales and cider, and a full licence was not granted until 1845. In addition to servicing the stage coach customers, it served for many years as a customs and excise staging post. But with the decline of the coaching era, it reverted to a wayside inn, with the stables used to store carriages and wagons.

The location of the Plough meant that it was built with no cellar. Even so, before the development of more robust defence systems, this pub was frequently flooded and entrances had to be raised – as can easily be seen by the flight of steps up to both doors in the photograph.

The Plough pictured during its – thankfully short – period of closure in 2013

In February 2013 the Plough, with mounting debts, closed its doors. This is hardly a new story but at least this one had a happy ending, for in September the same year it was purchased by a local consortium and now trades as a community pub.

Prince of Wales, Fairfield Road, New Romney TN28 8HW

The building that was until recently the Prince of Wales stands on the corner of Fairfield Road and George Lane. George Lane is a very old and attractive part of New Romney, and the three cottages that stand alongside the Prince of Wales all share its Grade II listed status.

The building itself is of early 19th century construction, and of two storeys. It started life as a domestic property and it is unclear just when it became a public house. By the latter part of the century it was providing B&B accommodation, although its clientele appears to have comprised mostly itinerants. Through the next century it was a popular back-street "local" with central fireplace and offered drinkers access to a small courtyard garden.

The Prince of Wales long held a reputation for eccentric diversification, with boot making and other services on offer in the 1950s and 1960s; and, up until very shortly before closure, it was still selling old fashioned sweets from glass jars behind the counter.

JOHN BARMAN

Boots & Shoes Repaired

+ + +

BEST MATERIAL, MODERATE PRICE

+ + +

Agent for A. & W. Mummery's Vegetable & Flower Seeds.

"Prince of Wales", NEW ROMNEY

But in the 21st century, the market for such out of the way public houses became very limited and the Prince of Wales closed its doors at the end of 2011. When it was put on the market in October 2012, planning permission had already been granted to return the Prince of Wales to a residential dwelling, which undoubtedly assisted its quick sale.

The Prince of Wales shortly after closure (left), and after conversion to a private dwelling (right)

Rose & Crown, 46–48 High St, New Romney TN28 8AT

The Rose & Crown has a rich history, and certainly predates the 18th century, when it was used (but not on an exclusive basis) for ceremonial purposes and Sessions Meetings. We know from both this background and smuggling histories that it was a large building with stabling behind: in 1743, following the landing of a huge "run", 150 smugglers took over both the Rose & Crown and the Dolphin and openly challenged the authorities to a confrontation. An observer at the time complained that this was the first time that the Rose & Crown's stables were so full that his own horse could not be accommodated. Not a lot is recorded of the Rose & Crown in the 20th century, and some references are erroneously to the pub of the same name at Old Romney. It seems to have closed in the 1950s. In recent years, the building has hosted a mobility shop and a taxi office, and in 2013 became home to Fish & Peri, an eastern European restaurant and grill. Part of this enterprise was rebranded as the Aboyne House Restaurant in 2014, apparently reflecting an informal name by which the pub was once also known.

The former Rose & Crown, pictured in 2013

Ship Hotel, 83 High Street, New Romney TN28 8AZ

The Ship, by virtue of its prominent position on the corner of the High Street and the Avenue, has always held significance within New Romney. It is steeped in history, even if there is some conflicting information. Although the façade is Georgian, the building significantly predates this time. The foundations are probably of 14th century origin, lending credibility to the Ship's claim of being one of the oldest buildings on the Marsh. Some sources

The Ship, 2013

even suggest that timbers found in the cellar may date back as far as 1000 AD, although others that it was built in 1492. Whatever the speculation, it is highly likely that the original building was constructed from ships' timbers from the port.

Exactly how long the Ship has traded is also open to some conjecture, although the first recorded keeper was Thomas Banne, described as an ostler of the parish of Romney, at some time in the 16th century. The pub is later mentioned in a will of 1579, when Samuel Dunstare bequeathed the inn and stables to his wife. It seemed that she enjoyed better health than her husband, as she kept it on for 31 years after his death.

In 1662 the inn underwent extensive alteration with the thatch, wattle and daub being largely removed and replaced with tiles and bricks. The present façade dates from 1728. In 1793, Elizabeth Rolfe (from a prominent Romney family, which still has links to the town) became landlady. By this time, the Ship was an established coaching halt on the main Rye to Dover route, and later (in 1802) became a timetabled stop on the route.

The Ship has had a colourful and varied past. Being the regular venue for coroner's courts does not mark it out as unusual, although this may well have caused some anxiety for other patrons, whose activities were not quite so legitimate, for it was regularly used by the organis-ers of unofficial sheep auctions and was also a favoured haunt of freetraders. The blocked-up doors within the cellar formerly linked to the network of smugglers' tunnels under the town. The Ship continued to hold prominence in the early and mid-20th century and for over a decade (from around 1910), a small cinema – operated by business partners Toner and Bloom – was installed within the concert room and proved to be extremely popular. During WWII, its cellar was used as a public air-raid shelter.

The Ship understandably and unashamedly trades on its traditions and stresses that its 15th (*sic*) century charm can still be witnessed in its wealth of oak beams and inglenook fireplace. The lounge area displays some original and period features, such as the brick fireplace; and the restaurant doubles as a function room. In literature, the Ship is the only one of New Romney's pubs to feature in Russell Thorndike's Doctor Syn saga – as an occasional haunt of Syn's henchman Mipps. It can also be fairly safely assumed that it was well known to the author himself.

The ownership of the Ship reflects that of many a Marsh hostelry, having passed through the hands of Friend, Mackeson and Whitbread before being acquired by Shepherd Neame in 1992. An unsavoury incident put it in the news headlines in 2012, in conjunction with a plot to rob the Nationwide cashpoint machine in New Romney High Street. The court heard that the conspirators met in the Ship to plan the raid (and later moved on to the Prince of Wales at Hythe).

Smugglers' Alehouse, St Lawrence Court, High Street, New Romney TN28 8BU

The newest entry in this book, the Smugglers' Alehouse is a micropub occupying a former tattoo parlour in the High Street. Opening in February 2006, it is jointly owned, with one of the partners having previously been involved in pub management in Folkestone. It is interesting that this opened at the time that the New Inn, a few doors along, was being sold. In this part of the High Street it does seem that small may be the way forward. The interior is decorated with pictures that recall the area's role in the smuggling trade.

Victoria Hotel & Posting House, 9–11 High Street, New Romney TN28 8BU

The Victoria was once a prosperous part of New Romney life. It became established in the 19th century, and by 1879 a prominent local figure – Mr J.J. Moody – had become landlord. Moody was also an omnibus proprietor and built up a thriving service, which included a thrice-weekly service from New Romney to the Metropole in Folkestone. The bus business was subsequently taken over by the well-known Carey Brothers in 1920, and later sold on to the East Kent Service in 1953. As with the New Inn, the Victoria was once the venue for both New Romney Cricket and Football Club meetings. Today, the former Victoria Hotel is home to a Chinese takeaway business.

This late 19th century photograph (left) shows proprietor J.J. Moody outside the Victoria Hotel in its heyday. On the right is the building in more recent use (2012)

The Warren Inn, Dymchurch Road, New Romney TN28 8UF

The first thing that most people notice about the Warren is its inn sign. And it is legitimate to question why the depiction is of a racehorse rather than a rabbit. The pub stands on reclaimed warren land, where the townsfolk previously kept rabbits for meat; but it was also the site of a racecourse of the same name where an annual meeting for a cup of gold plate took place in the 18th century. On older OS maps, a nearby bridge that crosses the dyke is marked as Horserace Bridge. "Warren" is actually a Roman term for an enclosure.

The Whitbread "miniature" reproduction of the Warren's inn sign (1950s, left); and the current (2014) sign (right)

There has been a pub on this site for well over 500 years, although the current building dates only from 1860. As with the Bell at Hythe and the Woolpack at Brookland, the sea formerly came up to the pub garden. It is still apparent that the building originally comprised two semi-detached properties, with only the right-hand weatherboarded part (as viewed from the road) initially dispensing alcohol.

The Warren Inn in 1905 (left) and in 2014, just after a refurbishment (right)

There are many interesting stories attached to the Warren, including that of two Norwegian sailors shipwrecked close by, in 1887. They turned up at the pub seeking refuge, which provoked no little interest. In the early part of the 20th century, the Warren was a regular meeting point for shooting parties; and in the 1940s, "roguers" (who had the job of removing "rogues" – weeds – from crops) would lodge here. During WWII, it was also popular with servicemen and ENSA would stage shows here.

Despite its popularity, by the 1950s the Warren remained a typical pub of the area, of pitch and tar with a dirt floor. The landlord at this time was a real character, widely known as "Flatcap Sid". He kept a donkey and a cat: he would regularly take the donkey upstairs, whilst the cat had a reputation for fighting anything that moved. During the time of Sid's tenancy – and when television was just starting to feature in people's lives – great excitement was caused by the appearance of *Opportunity Knocks* host Hughie Green, when he called in after landing at the nearby Ferryfield Airport.

Sid took his own life in one of the upstairs rooms, and it is said that he has since haunted the pub. Of all the claimed pub hauntings, this would seem to this author to be one of the most believable: the current landlady is convinced that Sid's presence is never far away, and she is a credible witness. There are no outlandish claims of sightings, but his presence is often felt by blonde girls (Sid isn't apparently attracted to brunettes or redheads) and there are lots of unexplained noises, particularly of footsteps. Items regularly go missing, only to turn up a few days later. Of particular note is that the landlady's wedding ring went missing one January day. After much searching, she had given up hope of seeing it again when, one evening – 10 months later – she joked to her barmaid that Sid had overstepped the mark this time and if he had any decency, he would return her ring. The next day, when opening the store cupboard (a cupboard she accessed up to 10 times a day), the ring was there, right next to the vacuum cleaner. Part of the legend is that Sid reacts particularly badly to any sign of change or modernisation, but he is presumably happy with the alterations made in March 2013 as he has not voiced any objection. At around this time, though, a small child asked about the black dog she had seen run through the garden fence. The pub didn't have any such animal, but the sighting followed the discovery of the bones of a large dog that had been uncovered whilst digging the flower beds.

Today, the Warren markets itself as a "friendly and cosy Victorian pub" and there is no reason to argue with that assessment. It remains popular and has been voted amongst the top five pubs in the county by listeners to Radio Kent, as well as winning Shepherd Neame local awards.

7

Marsh Borders

As advised in the introduction, the arbitrary criterion for inclusion within this section is that pubs – or at least the main part of the village they serve – should be within two miles of the generally accepted borders of Romney Marsh. Many of the villages that accommodate these pubs are just to the north of the Royal Military Canal, on the higher ground overlooking the Marsh. Such positions afforded good vantage points and also provided convenient staging posts for the storage and concealment of contraband. Accordingly, almost all have strong and credible links to smuggling.

Aldington

Aldington is a village steeped in history and, on a fine day, offers spectacular views across the Marsh to the sea. It is as the home of freetraders George Ransley and Cephas Quested of the infamous Aldington Gang that it is best known, but it was also the residence of the unfortunate Elizabeth Barton. She was the "Holy Maid of Kent", a poor servant girl who was prone to "visions", which brought her to the attention of King Henry VIII. In all likelihood, she suffered from epileptic fits, but when her prophesies began to anger the king, her fate was sealed and she was executed.

Walnut Tree Inn, Forge Hill, Aldington, Ashford TN25 7DT

The first known building on this site was in the 14th century, during the reign of Richard II, and was probably a one-roomed shack belonging to a looker (shepherd) or fisherman. By the 17th century it was known to be brewing beer, as a brew house was included in a 1687 inventory. But it was 1704 before a licence to sell ales and ciders was formally granted.

It was during the Napoleonic wars that the Walnut Tree became synonymous with the Aldington Gang, who made it their headquarters. Not exactly model patrons, they would think nothing of breaking in and helping themselves to food and drink outside of opening hours. Still visible is a small upstairs window overlooking the Marsh: this would be used to shine a light to signal to those controlling smuggling operations from Aldington Knoll. Tunnels (now unfortunately filled in) once led from the pub to both the church and houses on

191

The Walnut Tree in 2012

the edge of the Marsh – presumably central to smuggling operations. After industrial-scale smuggling came to an end, the pub continued its association with unsavoury activities by hosting cock fighting into the 20th century.

The colourful past of the Walnut Tree makes it a hotbed of ghostly activity, real or imagined. In addition to the murdered victims of the Aldington Gang and those smugglers summarily executed nearby, the kitchen lies over a burial site for Black Death victims and during renovations a skeleton was uncovered. Noises heard outside the pub on quiet winter nights have been attributed to a fight between members of the Hawkhurst gang (membership of these "rival" smuggling groups was not mutually exclusive). Legend had it that one combatant was killed and his body dragged to a well next to the pub, where it was disposed of.

Aldington Frith

In the *Ingoldsby Legends*, Richard Barham had the settlement as the meeting place for warlocks and witches, but you won't find much in any guide books about Aldington Frith. So small that it hardly justifies the term "hamlet", it comprises just a scattering of buildings (and a one-time shop) at a minor crossroad some mile and a half to the west of Aldington. However, one of these buildings has accommodated a pub of some vintage, with a pleasant beer garden.

The Good Intent, Frith Road, Aldington Frith TN25 7HQ

The Good Intent was named after a smuggling schooner that operated mostly out of Rye (but sometimes out of Dover). This vessel had space in its sail room and false bulkheads for the storage of contraband, with room for 147 kegs of brandy in each. Under the cabin deck, next to the coal store, were more concealed hiding places. It was captured in 1837 by the revenue cutter.

Records show the pub bearing its name operating in 1855, and being sold on in 1857. In its more recent history, it traded for a short time as the Black Rabbit[1] and closed in 2011 before being sold and then re-opening under its original name. Unfortunately, it closed again in 2014 and planning permission has been applied for to convert the Good Intent to retail, office or restaurant use.

The Good Intent c. 1940 (left) and 2012 (right)

Bilsington

Another village nestling on the edge of – and overlooking – Romney Marsh, Bilsington is a Saxon village recorded in the Domesday Book under the name of Bilsvitone. It is probably best known now for its Grade II listed historic 13th century church and the striking 58-feet high Cosway obelisk dedicated to a local landowner who lost his life in a coaching accident.

White Horse, The Cross, Bilsington, Ashford TN25 7JX

There is fairly strong evidence that the White Horse was trading by 1801, although it is often suggested that it became the village local only in 1851 (owing to its inclusion in the census of that year). Sited in the middle of the village, it was originally a block of three cottages.

---

1. Pubs of this name are usually quite old, traditionally reflecting "rabbets" or grooves associated with woodworking or stonemasonry; but in this case the name probably did refer to the wild animal.

The White Horse, 2014

Its location has meant that in recent years it has unashamedly had to sell itself to more than a local market but, with a 50-seater restaurant, this has not been a problem. The building itself is very attractive and boasts inglenook fireplaces and stone floors, and the pub has always strived to achieve a balance between the needs of its diners and drinkers. In the 1990s, it achieved an enviable reputation for its speciality Bilsington Pie dish (naturally enough, made from Romney Marsh lamb). It is also a popular refreshment point for those walking the Royal Military Canal and has a garden overlooking the Marsh.

Hamstreet

Described by Kent Life magazine as "interesting; and retaining the characteristics of a traditional and proud working village, something that is increasingly rare", in some parts of the county the village of Hamstreet is still known as "the Gateway to the Marsh". Served by the Hastings–Ashford rail line it is certainly a good point to start an exploration of the Marsh on foot, and three long-distance footpaths pass through the village.

Hamstreet achieved national prominence when maps of the village appeared on a series of postage stamps commemorating the Ordnance Survey in the 1990s. The village was chosen for this purpose because it was one of the first to be mapped as part of a national survey, and also because the changes to the village over time showed up well in such a representation. It also became the base camp for a spoof assault on the "mountainous" Romney Marsh by the Blue Peter children's television programme!

The village straddles two parishes: the majority of it lies within Orlestone, with a smaller part in Warehorne. For this reason, some sources state that Hamstreet has supported three pubs. But two of these – the Woolpack and the World's Wonder – are in Warehorne village and treated as such within this book.

Duke's Head (George/Three Mariners/Duke of Cumberland), The Street, Ham Street TN26 2HE

The Duke's Head has long held a prominent position in its community. The pub was originally known as The George and its front door opened directly onto the Street. It went through other incarnations – as The Three Mariners and the Duke of Cumberland – before taking on its present identity. It is first mentioned as the Duke's Head in *Pigot's Commercial Directory of 1832*. The same company's directory of 1840 records a daily van service connecting Hastings and Tenterden making scheduled stops outside.

From 1890, the pub was owned by Finn's of Lydd – one of their first forays outside the Marsh – and surviving photos show that the Duke's Head was home to at least one goal running team in the early part of the 20th century. The current mock-Tudor pub is, unsurprisingly, a rebuild dating from the 1930s. Its "twin" at Woodchurch (see Chapter 1) was sadly demolished in 2011.

The Duke's Head 1905 (left) and 2014 (below)

Iden

Mentioned in the Domesday Book, Iden started life as a clearing in the heavily-forested south of England and was once famed for its castle. It was home to Alexander Iden, who was reputedly responsible for the capture and slaying of the revolutionary Jack Cade. Unfortunately, all that now remains of the castle is its moat. Iden is often overlooked by tourists heading for Rye but it is a pleasant and attractive village, popular with walkers and cyclists, and where wild boar may sometimes be seen.

Bell Inn, Church Lane, Iden, Rye TN31 7PU

This country inn dates back, in parts, to 1107. Local legend has it that the original building was used as accommodation for the monks who built Iden church. It is also thought that there was once a tunnel between the pub cellar and the church. The pub retains an old-fashioned snug with open fire and it once had an outstanding garden. Unfortunately, when the pub was sold in 2007, the landlord of the time retained a large part of the original garden for development.

Mentioned in the novel *The Loves of Joanna Godden*,[2] the Bell allegedly accommodates two ghosts. It was at one time used to hold inquests and coroner's courts, and was mentioned in newspaper reports of 1842. These record that the court returned a unanimous verdict of wilful murder against some person or persons unknown after the discovery of the body of a

The Bell now has a much reduced garden (it once had its own paddock but a large part was sold off by a former landlord), although it still contains a fine example of an outside "privy" (2014)

---

2.   Author Sheila Kaye-Smith clearly had a penchant for pubs named the Bell, as that at Ivychurch also features in her book.

new-born girl. In 1857, the landlord was offering a stallion for stud (!) and four years later was in court accused of allowing gambling (specifically the playing of card games) on his premises. But the fact that the magistrate described him as of hitherto impeccable character suggests that this was a relatively well-to-do establishment.

The Bell was often a venue for the Romney Marsh Hunt and later – in 1999 – made national headlines after a BSE[3] health scare resulted in the government banning the sale of steak on the bone. Landlord Alan Coomber openly flouted the new law and invited public health officials to take action. This they duly did, and Coomber became the first Englishman to be charged under BSE legislation. In common with a number of pubs in the area, financial pressures resulted in the Bell's closure in around 2010, but it re-opened soon after. The adjacent stable block has been converted to offer accommodation to guests.

William the Conqueror, Main Street, Iden TN31 7PT

Iden is only a small village – currently of 400 residents – but in the 19th and 20th centuries it was not unusual for villages to have two pubs. Iden's other pub – the William the Conqueror – first appears by this name in a will and other documents of 1860 now held in the National Archives, although the building itself dates from the 18th century. In 1881, the landlord was additionally listed as being a saddler.

The pub has been mentioned in a number of accounts as hosting a ghost which sat at a spinning wheel in the front room. This, however, is inaccurate: the alleged haunting was at the Hayes Inn in nearby Northiam; the spinning wheel was subsequently moved to the William the Conqueror. In 1990 it rebranded itself as a pub bistro under the somewhat trendier name "Conkers" but, despite some short-term success, it closed in 1999. The licence lapsed in 2001 and, after 18 months trading as a bed and breakfast establishment, the building was sold on, reverting to private use.

The William the Conqueror at the turn of the 20th century (left) and now (right) in residential use (2014)

---

3. Colloquially known as "mad cow disease".

Lympne

Lympne is a small village sitting on the former sea cliffs overlooking the Marsh, with a significance at odds with its size. Important from early times for its commanding outlook over the coast and as a port (it was christened Portus Lemanis by the Romans), it was home to a Saxon shore fort and later Lympne Castle. The castle (dating back at least in parts to the 13th century) in more recent times served as a WWII observation post. It has now been fully restored and maintained and until recently was open to the public. Now a venue for corporate events and weddings, on a clear day the views from the grounds over Romney Marsh are unsurpassed. The village is also well known as home to the Port Lympne Wild Animal Park, established by the late John Aspinall.

County Members Inn, Aldington Road, Lympne, Hythe CT21 4LH

The County Members Inn is another pub that was initially three cottages subsequently knocked into one, although the timings of this are difficult to establish. It was certainly operating as a pub well before its first newspaper appearance in 1849, and a track running up from the Marsh and passing next to the building confirms its earlier smuggling credentials. Situated within an Area of Outstanding Natural Beauty (AONB), its location benefits it in terms of proximity to both the castle and the zoo.

There is some debate over the origin of the name. It may relate to the Trustees of the Cinque Ports, although most histories suggest that the inn was named after a number of prominent local MPs. There is, however, disagreement as to who these may have been, but we can

The County Members Inn in 2013 (right and bottom left) with (top left) an earlier pub sign from the 1960s

say with certainty (by virtue of its age) that none of them was Michael Howard. Nevertheless, the County Members achieved some national press coverage in 1995, as Howard's "local". Whilst this would not ordinarily be a major news story, Howard was Home Secretary at the time and had just repealed the draconian laws that had so severely restricted pub opening hours (and which had originally been introduced during WWI). Many newspapers at the time carried a photo of Howard emerging from the bar into the beer garden, a foaming pint in each hand.

Welcome Stranger, Court-at-Street, Lympne, Hythe CT21 4PF

The Welcome Stranger dated from 1820 and was purpose-built as an ale house, to serve a small rural community. It was not formally granted a wine licence until 1947, only obtaining a full licence some three years later. By no interpretation of the term can the pub have been described as financially successful, and it is a puzzle as to why Whitbread kept it on until 1974. At this point, the sitting tenant purchased it and it remained in operation as a free house. There is no indication that its fortunes improved as a result, although the quality of its ale was such that it managed inclusion within the Good Beer Guide of 1979.

However, it seems that landlord Drew Staunton – a known eccentric – became increasingly unpredictable in his ways, and selective in terms of both when he opened and whom he served. The pub suffered badly in the storm of 1987, with the roof seriously damaged and the sign blown down. Neither issue was addressed; the sign remained propped up against the wall and, to drink their beer, the friends of the by now reclusive landlord had to huddle in a corner of the main bar that was not exposed to the elements. To locals the Welcome Stranger became known as "the pub with no roof". Nevertheless, it continued to operate in this strange fashion right up until its final closure in 1993.

The Welcome Stranger in the early 1950s (photo: David Harper) and its 1951 Whitbread collectors' sign

The Welcome Stranger showing signs of decay in the late 1980s (photo: Michael Croxford – left). The rather functional houses (below) are on the site of the former pub, but recall the former use (by virtue of the name "Welcome Stranger Cottages")

This was by no means the end of the story, however. Despite ill-health, Mr Staunton remained in residence up until his death. He spent much of his time in a caravan on the site, but both this and the decaying main building brought him into conflict with the local planning authority (although permission had been given for the use of a mobile dwelling, it had not been positioned on the part of the estate specified). Mr Staunton died in 2003 and the property was sold the following year. After delays in securing planning permission (the building was listed) it was demolished in 2005 and housing – Welcome Stranger Cottages – erected on the site.

David Harper (*Whitbread: the Inn Behind the Signs*) relates an interesting anecdote about the Welcome Stranger from the 1950s. A three-piece band had been playing in the village but by the end of the evening there was some five feet of snow lying on the ground. The band sought refuge and stayed several days – notwithstanding that the landlord's food supplies extended to just one rasher of bacon for breakfast!

Newingreen

Not to be confused with Newing Green in another part of Kent (near Bromley), Newingreen is a fairly nondescript village standing on the junction of the A20 and the Roman Stone Street. Its location does make it ideal, however, for those travelling to or from the continent via Dover; using Lympne or Lydd airports; or visiting Canterbury, the Cinque Ports and (until recently) Folkestone racecourse. For this reason, it was once best known as the home of one of England's first motels. It is also now the global headquarters of the Holiday Extras company.

Royal Oak, Ashford Road, Newingreen, Hythe CT21 4JA

This low and elongated building standing at the junction of the Ashford, Folkestone and Hythe roads was once a coaching inn, and for a long time a very prominent and successful hostelry.

When it was under their ownership, Whitbread claimed that the building dated from 1560, but this is difficult to verify. Originally a farm building and drover's cottage, in 1775 it was purchased by a man called Caleb Buss, a farmer and brewer of Hythe. The following year, a limited licence was obtained, probably for the sale of home-brewed beer, and around this time significant modifications to the building were made, although it was not until 1797 that Buss's son Thomas successfully applied for a wine licence. At this time he also first registered the name of the Royal Oak. It must have been informally known by that name prior to this, as there are crime records showing a defendant claiming that he had bought a stolen horse at the Royal Oak as early as 1756. Some things never change over time! There are also records in smuggling literature of the notorious Ransley Gang visiting the pub after a "run" in March 1826.

Purchased by Mackeson's in December 1885, the Royal Oak was another of their establishments to have been linked to the John Jones Coursing Club. Later, it achieved national expo-

The Royal Oak, Newingreen in 1905 (left) and in current usage (2013 – right)

sure by becoming arguably the first motel built in England.[4] This gap in the market had first been spotted by a Canadian entrepreneur in 1953, who leased eight acres on which to build accommodation sleeping up to 50 guests and additionally housing ten garages. The project was taken forward by British hotel-keeper and architect Louis Erdi, and it immediately proved a hit with motorists breaking their journey on the way to the continent. To address changing demands and attitudes, in 1975 the garages were converted into one-bed units, and by 1987 the whole site upgraded to 27 chalet-style bedrooms. Unfortunately, changing travel habits led to reduced demand, and more stringent enforcement of drink driving laws made the restaurant side of the business less viable. Whitbread accordingly closed the motel in 1989 and sold the property.

A 1960 advertisement for the Royal Oak

Pleasingly, the fabric of the inn remains largely intact and fully recognisable. Holiday Extras purchased the site in 1999, and in 2001 a graphic, print and web design studio – Oak Creative – moved into the former pub accommodation. At this time the motel units, by now badly decayed, were found to have a high asbestos content, necessitating their destruction.

Playden

Playden village lies about a mile to the north of Rye. A visitor could be forgiven for passing by unaware of its existence, as the village has no obvious centre. There are no shops and the houses are scattered over the rural parish. Nevertheless, there has been a settlement in Playden since the New Stone Age. Playden – or Saltcote as it was then known – is mentioned in the Domesday Book and at one time had a thriving fish salting industry.

---

4. Some sources claim it was the second to be built, and this would seem more likely.

Peace & Plenty, Rye Road, Playden, Rye TN31 7UL

When the London–Rye Road was turnpiked in 1762, a tollgate and gatehouse were opened in Playden. Around the time of the Napoleonic Wars, a weatherboarded house was constructed next to the gatehouse and in the 1860s the owner opened this as a beerhouse, with a view to tapping into the turnpike trade. This was the Peace & Plenty, and can be seen to the right of the gatehouse in the photograph from 1872. With hindsight, the timing was unfortunate, as the arrival of the railway soon after resulted in a huge decrease in road traffic.

Newspaper reports of 1869 and 1876 recording prosecutions arising from assaults taking place there suggest that the Peace & Plenty was not then the refined place it later became.

The tollgate at Playden in 1872 with, on the far right, the Peace & Plenty

The Peace & Plenty featured in the 1950 Whitbread Inn Signs (second series; photograph on left by David Harper)

203

The Peace & Plenty in 2014, then operating only as a B&B business

Part of the original building was demolished in 1903 and a new front, which included a bar area, constructed shortly after. In 1954, half an acre of the site was taken for road widening; as part of the deal, East Sussex County Council erected a boundary fence and laid a paved car park for patrons.

Having attracted a reputation for good but expensive food, it closed as a pub around the turn of the 21st century, and then opened as an up-market bed & breakfast and restaurant establishment. Sadly, even this proved unsustainable and, whilst the B&B business continued, the restaurant closed to customers in 2014. Planning permission was granted for conversion back to private use later the same year, the final nail in the coffin of the Peace & Plenty.

Playden Oasts, Rye Road, Playden TN31 7UL

The Playden Oasts comprises three 19th century round oasthouses of red brick and tarred roof. With its walls covered in ivy, it makes a classic picture – underlining that the Sussex

The Playden Oasts, 2014

oasts can be just as impressive as their better-known Kent counterparts. Its interior walls are festooned with hops, a reminder of its former purpose, which it served until the late 1970s when it was converted to a hotel.

It further diversified because of the number of casual customers calling in for drinks: orders were taken, but only satisfied by sending a member of staff to the nearby Peace & Plenty with a tray! It is one of the more unusual pubs featured in this book and the owners have presented it to best advantage. Accordingly, the classic curves of the oast are not hidden; and a drink in the roundel bar – with its comforting log fire – can certainly make you realise that you are in historic surroundings. There are two separate restaurants and a large beer garden, as well as eight *en suite* rooms. Also unusual is that, until recently, the Playden Oasts offered guests the use of a private fishing lake, albeit situated some nine miles from the pub.

The Star, Scots Float, Military Road, Playden TN31 7PJ

The Star was one of the lesser known pubs in the area, sited on the Rye to Appledore Road. It was almost directly opposite Scots Float lock which – for obvious reasons – was formerly known as Star Lock (sometimes Starlock).

The building dates from the 18th century, although there is little evidence of it becoming a pub until the latter part of the following century. By 1900 (but in all probability much earlier) it was part of the Finn empire and formed part of the estate sold off to Style & Winch in 1921. For much of its life it was run by the Coleman family, who were also farmers. The pub's extensive land holding (useful for grazing) and number of bedrooms made it popular with drovers taking their flocks and cattle to and from Romney Marsh. It also had its own stables and boat house but, in spite of these advantages, it closed in 1953. The license was transferred

The Star in 1909 (above). The building to the right was the pub's own boathouse, whilst the outhouse on the left served mainly as a coal and wood store (picture: courtesy Bill Coleman). The picture (left) shows that the main building has changed little today

to the Inkerman Arms at Rye Harbour, and the building has since been in private use. The boathouse has now gone and the outbuildings have changed, but the main building remains quite recognisable.

Ruckinge

In common with other small villages on the northern edge of Romney Marsh, Ruckinge makes a claim to the notoriety of the Ransley Gang. But it is undoubtedly entitled to do so: George Ransley was born here (in 1792) and the village church contains the simple graves of some of his relatives. With fine views over the Marsh, Ruckinge is a pretty, if unremarkable, village.

Blue Anchor, Bilsington Road, Ruckinge, Ashford TN26 2NY

It is said that the Blue Anchor was originally opened partly to service a ship of the same name which was moored nearby. This is plausible; although now close to the Royal Military Canal, the village was formerly coastal and even after the land had been reclaimed there were still inlets stretching up to the village. It was certainly operating as a pub by 1799 as it features in trial transcripts of that year, William Ransley being found guilty of assaulting the landlord's wife. This incident also gives a pretty good indication of the type of clientele that the pub then attracted. Census records of 1851 show it to have been offering lodgings as well as ale (often a sign of a low-calibre establishment) by then. But, over the years, it became most respectable. By the mid-20th century it was offering three separate bar areas: a public bar (which incorporated darts and – later – a pool table); a snug; and a saloon bar, which later became a more formal restaurant. After subsequent conversion to an open-plan set up (but retaining its log-burning fireplace), the pub closed for a short time. However, its potential – with a good-sized beer garden, a patio overlooking a duck pond, and a two-acre field available for camping and caravanning – was not ignored and the Blue Anchor re-opened in 2012. Sold again in both 2013 and 2015, the new owner applied for change of use, to turn it into a community centre. At the end of 2015 the pub was closed and its future remains in doubt.

The Blue Anchor, 2014

Rye Foreign

Rye Foreign lies on the A268 road, to the west of Rye, and encompasses the hamlets of Bowler's Town and Springfield. Its name derives from the fact that Rye and Winchelsea were once under the jurisdiction of the Abbey of Fecamp in Normandy. Henry III looked to change this and signed a Charter of Resumption in 1247, bringing the two ports back under the King's control. But an area outside Rye remained under the control of the Abbey – and this became known as Rye Foreign.

Hare and Hounds, Rye Road, Rye Foreign, TN31 7ST

The Hare and Hounds was built in 1590, as a farm dwelling on a sizeable estate. At this time, it had a thatched roof and jettied upper storey. A hundred years later it had fallen into a very poor state of repair, necessitating extensive refurbishment. When this had been completed, it was purchased by a Peasmarsh brewer who, in 1703, successfully applied for a licence to sell ales and cider. By 1787 it had changed hands but remained as a pub, albeit with an extension, which was used to sell groceries. At this time it also first acquired the name of the Hare and Hounds. In 1895, the pub became part of Rye brewer John Bowen's estate, although it was not until it had passed through the hands of Alfred Leney & Co and the Star Brewery that, in 1938, the Hare and Hounds obtained a full licence.

Sitting in the middle of lovely countryside, the property boasts a large and child-friendly garden. In later years, however, the pub's location meant that it struggled. By necessity it had to build up the restaurant side of the business, but it was good to see that, in 2007, when temporarily closed, a planning application to convert to residential use was fiercely opposed by local residents intent that this part of their heritage should not disappear. Unfortunately, this was only a temprary reprieve. Although remaining very much unchanged externally, from 2014 it became solely a bed and breakfast establishment.

The Hare and Hounds c 1930 (above) and 2014 (right)

Royal Oak (Rumpels/Rumples; The Oak), Peasmarsh Road, Rye Foreign TN31 7SY

Following in the footsteps of the Royal Oak at Newingreen – co-incidentally in light of its subsequent name change – Rumpels became a motel in the late 1950s (its first telephone directory listing being in 1959). It also operated as a private members' club, but it is unknown for what the main building was used prior to that.

Dunkling & Wright (*Pub Names of Britain*) and Jacqueline Simpson (*Green Men and White Swans*) link the name to the fairy tale character Rumpelstiltskin. It is certainly the case that its sign did for a time depict this character, but some locals believe that it rather reflects the name of a Hampshire family that moved into this part of Sussex. This is also far from conclusive as the family name is Rump*les*. Rumpels did eventually become Rumples, but the reason for the change is also unclear (it has been suggested that the original name was merely a spelling mistake, perpetuated in subsequent listings).

The change to the Royal Oak came about when new owners took over in 2006. The same family had previously run the Royal Oak at Whatlington (near Hastings) and wished to retain the name in this new venture. They also brought a change of focus, too, and concentrated on building up the pub side of the business, whilst still maintaining the accommodation. Their efforts showed what could be done to a community pub, even with the challenge of so few houses around. They introduced an annual boules competition, a wassail[5] evening, their own

The Royal Oak, Rye Foreign (2014)

---

5. Wassailing (literally "howling" from the Anglo Saxon) is an ancient practice involving the pouring of cider on the roots and branches of apple trees and making loud noises to scare away any evil spirits in advance of the new harvest.

fun run and regular morris dancing, and even produced their own newsletter. They also built some new, smarter chalet accommodation units in the yard. By the end of the decade, this had become a dynamic and popular venue.

In 2015, after a short closure, The Royal Oak re-opened and was re-branded as The Oak, "a trendy English wine bar and restaurant". It is Grade II listed, with an attractive garden and patio area, and continues to provide ten units of motel accommodation – on a themed basis.

Rye Harbour

Despite being very much a "young" village, Rye Harbour is steeped in history. The village sits on a shingle beach near the estuary of the River Rother, almost two miles from the port of Rye.

Although there was a handful of dwellings prior to then, Rye Harbour was first significantly populated only in 1805 when a company of dragoons was based here during the Napoleonic Wars. Soon after, it began to be colonised by fishermen. When the threat of Napoleon had disappeared, resources were channelled into the war against smuggling and the Coast Blockade was established. At Rye Harbour, the striking Watch House was built in 1825 to provide a local base for the blockade.

What really put Rye Harbour on the map, however, was a tragedy in which 17 local lives were lost. This was the sinking of the *Mary Stanford* lifeboat in 1928. There were three generations of one family who perished, and barely a family in the village that was unaffected. The tragedy was compounded by the fact that the crew of the stricken vessel had already been rescued when the *Mary Stanford* put to sea, and the incident resulted in the rewriting of protocols regarding use of telegrams. The fine gothic-style local church has a permanent memorial to these brave men and an annual service in their memory still takes place. For more information, see *A Changing Shore* by Michael and Ruth Saville or http://marystanford.co.uk.

In the summer the place is bustling, with its own small fishing fleet and an impressive new lifeboat station. And despite accommodating a holiday village and industrial estate, the main village retains an old-fashioned charm. There is always much to do and see on the water and, at high tides, the channel can accommodate some very sizeable vessels (including the occasional paddle steamer). It additionally has its own nature reserve, with a network of footpaths and information centre, and which attracts 200,000 visitors a year.

Next to the huge public car park is Rye Harbour's own Martello Tower, and it is interesting to reflect that, when built only 200 years ago, this was actually on the beach (which is now more than half a mile away). Possibly best known to generations as "Westling" in Monica Edwards' children's books, this small settlement also once had its own railway branch line (for industrial purposes) and has surprisingly supported three pubs, two of which remain.

Inkerman Arms, Harbour Road, Rye Harbour TN31 7TQ

This traditional freehouse dates back to around 1860 at the time that Inkerman Terrace was built, the name reflecting the Crimean War battle which took place in 1854.[6] There is some mystery in that, in 1953, the licence from the Star at Playden was transferred here, strongly suggesting that at the time the Inkerman had only a restricted (rather than full) licence. It now comprises a spacious main bar with wood-burner fire and a picturesque beer garden, which also has its own boules piste.

The Inkerman Arms, 2014

The Ship, The Point, Rye Harbour TN31 7TU

The first of Rye Harbour's pubs, it is generally reported that the Ship was established some time in the 1840s, built as part of a general development, which included a few houses and a shop. This development reflected the good employment prospects for all in Rye Harbour at this time, whether on cargo boats or in the fishing industry (not only through the fishing fleet but also in terms of keddlenet fishing, shrimping and the harvesting of oysters). However, there have been claims that The Ship predated the other buildings and that it may even have been built as early as 1795. If that is the case, it would almost certainly be the oldest property in the village.

As the only public house in the area at the time, The Ship was the venue for inquests, one of which was held in April 1854. This was a very sad affair as it involved the body of a baby that had been discovered in undergrowth by a dog. The surgeon concluded that the child had

---

6. A number of pubs of this vintage bear this name, the scene of a dramatic British (and allied) victory.

been born "with assistance" but strangled shortly after. Presumably the baby and mother must have been local, but it seems that nobody came forward either at the time or later, and the verdict was one of murder by person(s) unknown.

The sale of the Ship at the end of the 19th century to a Mrs Lucas Shadwell was, unfortunately, the pub's death knell. The Lucas Shadwells, who lived in Fairlight Hall, were huge landowners (their ownership extended to most of the land between Rye Harbour and Fairlight) and also generous benefactors. In addition to funding the building of the Rye Harbour church, the family also paid for the construction of the vicarage and were to help out in times of unemployment. But a significant downside (as far as this author is concerned) is that they were actively involved in the temperance movement, and were responsible for closing down numerous pubs in the area.[7] The Ship was bought specifically for this purpose. It has ever since been in use as a private dwelling.

Ship Cottage (left) in 2014. It is believed that No. 2 Ship Cottages (right) was at one time an annex to the pub

William the Conqueror, Rye Harbour TN31 7TU

Sitting on the bank of the River Rother, records show that this was originally a fisherman's cottage, dating to the establishment of the village (i.e. around the start of the 19th century). Claims have been made that it opened as a pub at about the same time as the Inkerman

---

7. Although the temperance movement in Rye was strong, it seems that Mrs Lucas Shadwell was a rather late convert. The family opposition was not rooted in religious belief but related, at least partly, to an incident at a pub in Pett where a delivery driver acting on behalf of the family had popped in for a quick refreshment without securing his horse and cart. The horse bolted, and collided with a small boy, the Rector's son, who subsequently died of his injuries.

Arms, but there is little to support them. It could conceivably have been a minor beerhouse at the time, but later records show that, following sale in 1891, it opened as a pub the next year – comprising part of the Tenterden Brewery estate. Offered for auction in 1921, it was described as the only licensed house in the district, acknowledging the limited status of the Inkerman Arms at this point. But this distinction did not result in any buyers coming forward at the time, and instead it was bought by brewers Jude Hanbury the following year.

The location of the William the Conqueror (WTC) – and indeed the village of Rye Harbour itself – undoubtedly lent itself to the free trade. Whilst the building was constructed after the "golden age" of smuggling, there was still much activity in the area and there are several reliable accounts that place the WTC very much at its centre – despite the inconvenient presence of the Watch House nearby.

In August 1940, the pub was requisitioned by the War Office and closed down, to reopen in August 1945 under the same licensee. In the 1950s, a ferry service ran from Rye Harbour to Camber and the regular ferryman, Johnny Doughty, was a WTC regular. A veritable larger-than-life character, "Uncle Johnny" would often sing songs to entertain the regulars as he waited in the pub between crossings. Unfortunately, the reliability of the ferry service tended to deteriorate as the day wore on!

The WTC remained a traditional and basic pub for many years, before undergoing a major makeover by brewers Shepherd Neame in early 2016. There remains a long bar known as the Mess Room, containing a forged iron screen showing a Norman on horseback wielding a war axe. Outside is a WWII mine used to collect money for distressed mariners.

The William the Conqueror, pictured just after WWII (left) and in 2012 (right)

Saltwood

Saltwood, a mile inland from Hythe, above the cinque port, has been described as a typical Kentish village. The village today is centred around the village green, but Saltwood is probably best known for its castle which dates from 1160. This was where the 1170 plot to assassinate Thomas Beckett was hatched – King Henry having famously asked who could rid him of this "turbulent priest". More recently, it has been known as home to the late outspoken and maverick Alan Clark MP (whose father was the well-known historian and author Sir Kenneth Clark).

Castle Hotel, The Green, Saltwood, Hythe CT21 4AJ

Parts of the fabric of this building date back to the 1800s, when it comprised three adjacent cottages. These were built for retainers of important visitors to Saltwood Castle, after it had been restored to once again provide a home (one of several) for the Archbishop of Canterbury.

The Castle is a large, imposing building overlooking the village green, now with a late Regency appearance. It has always been the hub of village life, and as much a pub as a hotel. In 1947 it was offering patrons a sitting room, coffee room, saloon and public bar. In 1957, Mackeson purchased the attractive village pond in front of the pub, which was concreted over to form a car park. Later, the public and saloon bars were combined.

The Saltwood Castle, 2014

Sandgate

Located between Folkestone and Hythe, the coastal village of Sandgate is easily overlooked by the motorist passing through. But it offers good beaches with views over the Channel and is popular for its antiques shops and boutiques. It also at one time had its own brewery, established in 1836 by Robert Hills of Lympne, close to the Clarendon Inn. This eventually ended up under the control of the Mackeson brothers and cottages now stand on the site.

Its location means that Sandgate has been in the front line against invasion and the numerous Martello Towers in the vicinity were preceded by a castle on the pebble shore. This was built in the reign of Henry VIII, but has been re-fortified over the years as part of updated defence precautions. A major storm in 1950 and coastal erosion caused severe damage, but the castle has been fully repaired and is now privately owned – albeit somewhat different in appearance from its original form.[8] The village itself has been subject to landslips and one such in 1893 caused widespread structural damage.

Sandgate has for long been synonymous with the army, and the Shorncliffe Camp was established here in 1794. Although the Light Infantry vacated in October 1986, it is now the home to the Royal Gurkha Rifles.

The town was also the birthplace of comedy actress Hattie Jacques and sometime home to author HG Wells. Wells moved here towards the end of the 19th century for health reasons, and Sandgate at that time has been described as "the world's literary centre". This is quite a claim and probably owes much to an enterprising tourist board. For whilst authors such as Joseph Conrad, Henry James, Ford Madox Ford and Edith Nesbitt may have been seen in the vicinity, none of them actually lived here; Rye would have had a more legitimate claim to such a title. But Sandgate was undoubtedly popular with visitors, who also included George Bernard Shaw, Arnold Bennett, Sir James Barrie and politicians such as Winston Churchill (who was a friend of local MP Edward Sassoon).

Whether a coincidence or not, Sandgate has been incredibly well-blessed in terms of drinking establishments, particularly in the 19th century, although many of these were beerhouses – some of which had only a short life – and a number of which had similar names. These included eight that opened in the 1850s: the **Allied Arms**,[9] which had disappeared by 1866; the **Alma** which closed in 1858; the **City** and the **Flower Pot**, both of which closed in 1869 after about ten years of service; the **British Flag**, which had closed by 1871; the **Prince of Wales** (formerly the **Inkerman Arms**), which operated between c. 1858 and 1869; the **Duke of Cambridge**, which lasted around a dozen years; and the **Union**, which survived only about five years but earned a very unfortunate reputation (for squalor and prostitution) in its short life. The **Victoria Beerhouse** probably did not open until very early in the 1860s, but closed by the end of the same decade. Others which were more enduring, but are nevertheless

---

8. One glaring alteration being the addition of a stainless steel cap on the main keep.
9. As previously, pubs set in bold type do not have separate entry in the book.

no longer with us, were the **Castle Tavern**, which started life as the **Martello Tower** around 1805 and survived to 1911;[10] and the **Rose Inn**, which was well established by the mid-19th century and which eventually closed in 1968. Predating all of these was the **Bricklayers Hotel**, which opened in the mid-1820s and closed at the outbreak of WWI (by which time it had transformed into the **Alexandra Hotel & Alhambra Theatre**); and the **Duke of York**, which closed in 1911 after almost 100 years' service. All of the above-named would appear to have been situated in the High Street, although there is debate as to the exact location of some of them.[11] However, the prize for longevity goes to another High Street pub, the **Fleur de Lis**, which, when it closed in 1974, had probably notched up 250 years' service. Running it close would be another High Street establishment, the **Royal Kent Hotel and Tap**[12] (formerly the **New Inn**), which ran from 1775 to 1962. This occupied numbers 79 to 83.

And yet even the above long list does not cover all of the High Street's known pubs. There were at least two more: the **Victoria Tavern** (c1830–1871); and the **Marine Hotel** (1838–1862). Away from the High Street there were not quite so many, but the rest of Sandgate was hardly a desert either. The **Military Tavern** (1868–1963), but more commonly known locally as the **Hole in the Wall**, stood in Military Road and was a significant and popular pub. When this closed, its landlord jumped ship to the nearby Fleur de Lis and the building was bulldozed soon after.[13] In addition to a number of short-lived hotels, other pubs and beerhouses have included:

- **The Duke of Wellington** (c1841–1869) – a beerhouse in Chapel Street;
- **The Good Intent** – a beerhouse which operated from around 1838 to 1865 and was probably sited in Castle Road;
- **The Old Trotting Horse** – a Castle Green alehouse that traded for about a dozen years either side of the turn of the 19th century;
- **Plates & Basins** – a beerhouse that closed in 1863, but location unknown;
- **Rose Tavern** – a very short-lived 18th century alehouse located in Prospect Road;
- **The Royal Oak** – a beerhouse opening in the Upper Folkestone Road (Sandgate Hill) in the mid-1860s and subsequently trading under a full licence until closure in 1973;
- **The Sandgate House** – location unknown but recorded as being closed in 1717; and
- **The True Briton** – yet another beerhouse in Chapel Street which opened in the 1850s as the **Duke of Cumberland**, and survived just over a decade.

Now Sandgate has only three traditional pubs and two hotels open to the public, although the drinking scene is augmented by a number of bars, catering to the younger market, including

---

10. This may have also traded at one time as the **Sandgate Fort**. The Sandgate Fort is mentioned in 1765 records, but it is unclear whether it was an alehouse in its own right .
11. It has been suggested that the Alma and Duke of Cambridge may have been elsewhere in the town, but the balance of probabilities is that they were in the High Street.
12. The term "tap" in the context of a hotel usually denoted a licensed premises attached to the enterprise, often popular with the working classes (as, for example, the George at Rye).
13. The site is now part of a small public gardens.

the **Bar Vasa** on the Esplanade. And in October 2015 a new micro pub – the **Inn Doors** – opened for business, at 96 High Street.

Clarendon Inn/Earl of Clarendon, Brewers Hill,[14] Sandgate CT20 3DH

The clifftop location of the Clarendon offers spectacular views over the English Channel (even to France on the clearest of days) and comes into its own when the seas are rough and the fires are lit. It is generally believed that the pub started life as the Rose Tavern[15] in 1820 and from inception was popular with troops from the nearby barracks. By the time of its first recorded landlord in 1873, it had become the Clarendon Inn, although probably more hotel than inn (notwithstanding its compact nature). It was also the "tap" for the adjacent Sandgate Brewery. The new name commemorated Lord Clarendon, a former Warden of the Cinque Ports, who was responsible for the transformation of Sandgate from fishing village to seaside resort.

Although the Clarendon survived the 1893 landslip, it did move several inches, which resulted in severe cracking of walls and the destruction of kitchen equipment. In 1912 it was acquired by Mackesons. In October 2009, the pub was re-named the Earl of Clarendon. It has won CAMRA local pub of the year awards and is allegedly home to a poltergeist that seems to have a particular hostility towards microwave ovens – possibly linked to the 1893 incident!

The Clarendon Inn in the 1950s (left; photograph by David Harper); and as the Earl of Clarendon in 2014 (right)

14. Formerly Camp Road.
15. There are records of more than one pub of this or similar name in the town.

Gate 28, 28 High Street, Sandgate CT20 3AP

Gate 28 was opened in 1999 by a couple of young local graduates who had spotted a gap in the market. In this case, it was the 2000 staff employed in the locality by Saga, and for whom there were few other alternative lunchtime venues. With a modern and minimalist approach to furnishing and with live music at weekends, it was also popular with the younger generation. It closed in 2009 and the premises are now occupied by Escondido, a Mexican restaurant.

Providence Inn, 47–49 High Street, Sandgate CT20 3AH

Originally comprising just 49 High Street, it is unclear exactly when the Providence first became licensed as a beerhouse. *Pigot's Directory for 1826* shows the premises occupied by a butcher, John Elgar; by 1838 the listing shows him as additionally being a beer retailer. In the 1850s, the local health board ordered him to stop the slaughtering of cattle within his yard, which gives a clue to the fact that this was not the classiest establishment. Whilst a wine licence was obtained in 1948, it was not until 1953 that a full licence was issued. This was at the time that John Latchford had become licensee; and the pub was to remain in the same family until 2013. In the 1970s, the pub expanded by taking over the adjacent Sea Breeze café.

The Providence has for long been a popular pub with a friendly atmosphere. When the Latchford family felt unable to continue after 60 years in charge and took the decision to close the pub, it is said that – on the day of closure – some locals really did cry into their drinks. The landlord cited a not unfamiliar combination of the recession, increased rent and parking restrictions, for closure. However, a new landlord stepped forward and the pub re-opened after just a week.

The Providence Inn at the turn of the 20th century (left) and in 2011 (right; © Chris Whippett, licensed for reuse under a Creative Commons Licence)

Royal Norfolk Hotel, 7 High Street, Sandgate CT20 3BD

There was a pub on this site from the early 19th century when it was known as The Ship – one of two of that name within a very short distance of each other on Sandgate High Street. It changed its name following a visit by the Duchess of Norfolk in the latter part of the same century and has the advantage of overlooking Henry VIII's castle. There are a couple of incidents that feature prominently in the hotel's history. The first was a fight in 1825, which resulted in the death of one of the combatants. The other died soon after and a series of strange (allegedly "ghostly") subsequent events – which even resulted in the hotel staying empty for a number of years – were attributed to this. The other claim made by the hotel's owners was that Queen Victoria once visited. Whatever the truth of either incident, they do not apply to the current building; it was rebuilt in 1901 and the hauntings ceased.

In 1999, responding to changing demand, the hotel turned over most of its ground floor to accommodate a discrete public bar, named **Gees**.

Sandgate Hotel, 8–9 Wellington Terrace, The Esplanade, Sandgate CT20 3DY

First listed in 1978, the Sandgate Hotel had a small bar open to the public but existed primarily on paying guests and its restaurant business. It was fairly anonymous for much of its life, but this changed in 2006 when it featured in reality TV show *Gordon Ramsay's Kitchen Nightmares*. This was typically confrontational, with Ramsay being scathing of the management of the business. His visit failed to turn it around, however, and the then owners left the catering industry and sold the hotel. Under new ownership it is now flourishing, with two separate bars and fine sea views from the terrace. In addition to live music nights, it also hosts comedy club evenings and offers the attraction of coal fires in the winter months.

The Ship, 65 High Street, Sandgate CT20 3AH

It is difficult to establish just when the Ship first opened its doors, but, when the Shorncliffe Camp was constructed in 1794, the Ship was the pub of choice for soldiers stationed here to fight the Napoleonic Wars. It was also popular during a subsequent conflict, when the British German Legion (a group of German soldiers recruited to fight for Britain in the Crimean War) was formed and camped nearby. In the 1920s, under landlord Henry Beer, it rather immodestly styled itself as "the World Famous Ship Inn, Sandgate".

Another of Sandgate's pubs that backs onto the sea, the Ship has built onto its fortunate location by constructing a roof terrace for *al fresco* dining; this was completed in 2010. The pub claims to be haunted by two ghosts; one is a (rather predictable) soldier in Victorian uniform, whilst the other is more unusual. She is known as "the Fish Lady", as her presence is manifested by the rather unpleasant smell of rotting fish.

Prominent pub historians Martin Easdown and Eamonn Rooney have presented a convincing case that the **Sebastopol** – a beerhouse known to have existed for about a quarter of the 19th century – may well have operated out of the back bar of the Ship Inn. In 2015, the Ship became a brewpub, with the incorporation of a small brewery (the Amazing Brewery).

The Ship, 2014

Seabrook

Seabrook is a small settlement on the A259 between Hythe and Sandgate, marking the eastern end of the Royal Military Canal. Whilst it is has been administered from Hythe since 1886, it remains part of the parish of Cheriton. Many sources include the Britannia amongst its current pubs; to add to the confusion this is technically within the hamlet of Shorncliffe (and within this book features in the chapter on Hythe pubs).

Fountain Inn, 171 Seabrook Road, Seabrook CT21 5RT

The Fountain was first mentioned in the 1841 census and the only other surviving records of the original building show that it was acquired by Leney & Co in 1884 for £2,000, before being demolished in 1887–88. The demolition uncovered a stone salamander and a cannonball!

Rebuilt on the same site, it has served continuously as a pub ever since, with the exception of a four-month period from March 2013 when it shut as a result of the flooding of its cellar and bar. Heavy rain led to waist-deep flooding in Horn Street and Seabrook Road and a dozen customers had to be ferried to safety in an inflatable boat. The basement and ground floor suffered severe damage and some stock was ruined. Previously, in the 1950s, the local rector was in the habit of holding harvest festival services in the bar; customers would supply food items whilst the landlord donated the beer.

In recent years, the Fountain has built up its food trade and now boasts a large restaurant. It also benefits from both a large garden and a car park.

The Fountain (c1950, above; picture courtesy Kent Messenger) and in 2013 (right)

Royal Oak, Seabrook Road, Seabrook

The Royal Oak stood on the junction of Seabrook Road and Beacon Terrace and operated for only a short time in the mid-19th century. This small beerhouse was a family-run business that probably existed between 1838 and 1871. It seems likely that Seabrook also boasted another beerhouse located nearby. This is recorded in the 1850s, but details are sketchy.

Sea View Hotel/Seabrook Hotel, 95 Seabrook Road, Seabrook CT21 5QP

Built in 1888–89 and initially known as the Sandgate Hotel for a short time, the building was extended in 1906. After being taken over by Whitbread, this extension became home to the Seabrook Tap with separate entrance and inn sign (depicting a jovial sailor).

For much of its life, the Sea View Hotel attracted holidaymakers, business travellers and – because of its full licence – many locals. In 1961, it was renamed the Seabrook Hotel. By the late 1980s, it had been converted to a restaurant, trading as "Frederick's". Soon after, it enjoyed an equally short incarnation as the **Hythe Regency Hotel** before closing its doors. The building re-opened as a Christian Centre in November 1994 under yet another new name – Cautley House.

The Seaview Hotel, in the 1920s (above) and barely changed in nearly a hundred years (right, as Cautley House, 2014)

Stone-in-Oxney

Stone-in-Oxney is situated within an Area of Outstanding Natural Beauty just to the north of the Royal Military Canal and east of Rye. The stone to which the village name refers is of Roman origin and preserved in the altar of St Mary's, the village church. Although many guidebooks state that the depiction on the stone is of Mithras, it is more likely to be that of Apis (another figure from Greek mythology). It is believed to have been moved here from Stutfall Castle, where a Roman garrison was once based.

Crown Inn, Stone-in-Oxney, Tenterden TN30 7JN

Like many genuinely old pubs, it is difficult to date the Crown with any precision, but the oak beams and inglenook suggest that parts, at least, date back to the 17th century or earlier.

In the 1990s this was a popular pub, eschewing jukeboxes and electronic gaming machines in favour of vegetarian menus and jazz evenings. But the lack of houses in the area and an increasingly crowded and competitive marketplace meant it began to struggle and it has closed more than once since.

After closing its doors seemingly for good, it nevertheless reopened once again in 2008 as an up-market country bistro, with limited bed and breakfast facilities in addition; and in 2011 was nominated by *The Times* as "one of the best places for Sunday lunch and to spend a weekend".

The Crown's inn sign may still be traditional, but the target audience has certainly changed (2014)

Ferry Inn, Appledore Road, Stone-in-Oxney, Tenterden TN30 7JY

The Ferry Inn, built in 1690, was at one time known as the Tollgate and is still known to some of its regulars by the alternative informal name of the "Oxney Ferry".

Whereas many inland pubs on the marsh were at one time on the coast, the Ferry was on the southern edge of the former course of the River Rother, which has been diverted a number of times since by storms and reclamation. Built as it was to serve the needs of travellers crossing over the outlet of the River Rother to the mainland, the changing geography removed the inn's *raison d'etre*. Although still on the banks of a watercourse, this is now the attractive but less impressive Reading Street Sewer. A haven for wildlife, you could now almost jump this in parts, whereas the River Rother was a quarter of a mile wide here at one time. The coastline was formerly near to where the Military Road and Royal Military Canal are today (heading on the Military Road towards Appledore there is a striking example of an inland cliff), and evidence of the retreat of the sea is more visible here than on the Marsh. But the siting of the Ferry meant that it was very useful to those involved in the free trade and records confirm that it was popular with smugglers. Furthermore, there is an owler's window (by the inglenook in the corner of the main bar), which commands good views of the land and from which messages could be passed to indicate whether or not it was safe to land contraband.

During the Napoleonic Wars, troops were quartered here, in upstairs rooms and in the attic. The confined space in which they found themselves inevitably led to tensions and fights were not uncommon. One of these was particularly brutal – although this time the argument was over a woman – and resulted in the murder of one soldier by another (the killer subsequently being executed, at Chatham).

The Ferry Inn has passed through many hands over the years. Originally a free house, it was for a time owned by the famous Deedes family of Hythe and subsequently purchased by Edwin Finn of Lydd. Finn in turn leased it to another local brewer – Style and Winch – who later purchased it outright. Courage Barclay Simmonds (later Courage) bought out Style and Winch in 1953, but later sold the Ferry and it remains a free house today. It retains a schedule of ferry charges at the front of the pub, which also has an attractive forecourt.

The Ferry Inn c. 1900 (photo: courtesy Ted Carpenter)

224

Warehorne

First mentioned in 820, Warehorne is a corruption of the village's original name of Werehornas, meaning "the place on the bend by the weir". In all likelihood the weir would have been on the River Limen (the former name of the Rother, prior to nature's rerouting of it) although the Medway and Stour also have sources nearby. Like many villages on and around the Romney Marsh, it has a fine church of which it is justifiably proud. Although mentioned in the Domesday Book, however, the current Saint Matthew's – whilst undoubtedly old with parts dating back to the 13th century – is a later incarnation. For many years the village has been served by two pubs, one at either end. Although both closed in 2014, one reopened the following year.

Woolpack, Church Lane, Warehorne TN26 2LL

There are no prizes for guessing that a pub in this part of the world called the Woolpack was at one time a smugglers' haunt. This one dates back to the mid-16th century (when it was probably a farmhouse) and, like its namesake at Brookland, has some tangible reminders of its former connections. These include numerous trap doors with interconnecting passages and a flap in the porch through which smugglers could deposit their goods if being pursued by the authorities. There are stories of a smugglers' tunnel once linking the pub to the nearby church. Such tales are often open to question, but in this case provenance has been reasonably well evidenced; a former landlord admits to pouring concrete into the tunnel, and utility companies have unwittingly dug into other parts of it.

The Woolpack, 2012

The Woolpack shares its premises with numerous ghosts, and paranormal investigators in 2008 reputedly made contact with smugglers, a clergyman and a young girl. Also alleged to haunt the pub is a former landlord with a liking for barmaids, who by all accounts would also be of interest to the police if he was operating in the real world!

It is an all too common story, but the remote location of the Woolpack resulted in the pub struggling throughout the early 21st century. Closed in 2014, it was acquired by the same company now running the Globe Marsh at Rye,[16] and reopened for business in May 2015.

World's Wonder, Kenardington Road, Warehorne TN26 2LU

As already established, the World's Wonder was within the parish of Hamstreet. To add to the confusion, it was nearer to Kenardington than Warehorne, whose postal address it took. The pub dated from around 1860, when the Parish Council decided to sell a pair of adjoining cottages. The sale was by sealed-bid auction and the successful bidder was Thomas Knight, a local man of apparently only modest means. There was much speculation about where Knight could have acquired the money for this purchase. When he also told all and sundry that he was going to apply for a justices' licence (to open a beerhouse), there was further conjecture as to whether such a licence would be granted; and, if so, what the place would be called. Being by all accounts a mischievous fellow, Knight kept everybody guessing and finally declared that, because "all the world's been a wonderin'", that it would only be appropriate to

The original World's Wonder, 1890

16. And also the Five Bells at Brabourne.

name it the World's Wonder. To create a large enough beerhouse to be viable, however, he had to knock the two cottages into one.

In 1932, after being acquired by Style & Winch, the original building was demolished and replaced with a Dutch Barn-type construction – just as was the Ship Inn at Lade (see Chapter 2).[17] This was later slightly modified and extended. Whilst the rebuild was taking place, landlord Jimmy Homewood refused to close the business and, for over six months, dispensed beer, wines and food from an adjoining garage. The remote location of the World's Wonder means that it was for long heavily reliant on visiting trade and, despite strenuous marketing events by a number of landlords – including radical development of the restaurant side of the business – the pub became no longer viable in 2014. After a spell of opening only at weekends, it closed its doors for good at the end of that August.

The World's Wonder pictured just a week before closure. The sign depicted an extinct species of chicken, but did not reflect the true origin of the pub name. Note how similar this building is to another extinct pub: the Ship at Lade

---

17. Three other Style & Winch pubs were also built to the same design at this time: the Bell Inn at Coxheath (now closed); the Redstart Inn at Barming (near Maidstone); and the Papermaker's Arms (Hawley, near Dartford).

Appendix I

Terminology

The various terms used to describe England's drinking establishments have changed over the years, and have also been subject to local and regional variations. The following are the most generally – but not universally – accepted definitions:

Tavern

Taverns were the classic Roman drinking and social centres, the modern term being a corruption of the Latin word "tabernae". In Roman times the only alcohol served was wine and, although they later diversified, this remained the stock-in-trade for many *bona fide* taverns. As wine was for a long time more expensive than most other drinks, this meant that they tended to cater for the wealthier members of society. Taverns have always served food and for the most part been restricted to towns. Never that prevalent, they were vastly outnumbered by alehouses. In the 18th century, a number were converted to coffee houses in order to continue to serve the more affluent classes.

Alehouse

This is a generic term, which became widely used in mediaeval times, when it referred to an ordinary dwelling where the owner or tenant served home-brewed ale (which was then brewed without hops). In some cases, the householder would call on the services of travelling brewers to assist him. Later, the term included those houses selling cider on the same basis and, later still, some alehouses started serving food, while still being known by the same name. Initially, many alehouses simply dispensed alcohol from their own front room. Over time, those alehouse owners who were successful were able to buy an adjoining property, into which they would move their families, which allowed them to expand the operation. Further expansion was also not uncommon and, by the mid-18th century, larger alehouses were becoming common and the term was increasingly replaced by the more generic public house or "pub". However, many alehouses never achieved (or even sought) the fuller licensing certificate that would allow them to be legally classified as a public house. Generally, alehouses would be licensed by local magistrates, and be subject to *ad hoc* inspection to confirm compliance with the terms of the licence.

Inn

Traditionally, inns were purpose-built establishments for the accommodation of travellers. They were far larger than the average house because of the need for more bedrooms and for stabling. They provided food as well as drink. The major inns of the day were constructed by monasteries in locations used by pilgrims. Others served military needs.

During the 18th century, those inns conveniently placed to take account of the increase in road traffic were able to expand, and new purpose-built coaching inns sprang up to take advantage of transport innovations. Sometimes the suffix "inn" was misleadingly added in an attempt to improve the standing of an alehouse, or where the accommodation on offer was no better than that of the cheapest lodging house.

Public house

It is often claimed that the term "public house" was first used in the 17th century. However, whilst it did not come into widespread usage until the following century, there is evidence of it being used in the late 1500s. It was generally used as a collective term to describe taverns, inns and the larger alehouses (and such an approach is reflected within this book). It was only from the mid-19th century that the public house came to be defined as an establishment that was licensed to sell a full range of alcoholic drinks to members of the public. This definition largely holds true today, although some bigger hotels are excluded from this interpretation.

It was also around the mid-19th century that the larger brewers started to construct purpose-built properties for the sale of wines, beers and spirits. These usually had numerous rooms catering to different social classes (reflecting the divisions that had been created by the stage and railway companies) and from the outset these were known as public houses. "Pubs", as they inevitably became colloquially called, were required to be licensed by local magistrates and could be (and were) inspected by the police at any time.

Beerhouse

"Beerhouse" was a term that took its name directly from the 1830 Beer Act, and was simply and legally defined as a place where beer (and cider) was sold to be consumed on the premises. Spirits and wines were specifically excluded. All proprietors had to do was purchase a licence from the government, costing two guineas a year (about £160 in today's money). At that time, there was no involvement of local magistrates, although this would later change.

In the majority of cases the beer would be brewed on the premises, but this was not exclusively the case. Beerhouses were sometimes also known as "small beer" or "Tom and Jerry" shops. Many beerhouses had only a short existence, whilst others became the haunt of criminals and prostitutes. Some, however, flourished and, in time, successfully applied for licenses that gave them full public house status. Indeed, a significant number of our current pubs started life as beerhouses.

Hotel

The term "hotel" was little used before 1800, the first such establishment (the Royal Clarence Hotel in Exeter[1]) not being opened until 1768. The generally accepted definition has for long been that of a commercial establishment that provides accommodation, meals and other services. A more recent legal definition is that it must have a minimum of six rooms for letting, at least three of which should be *en suite*. From the early 20th century, larger hotels have often incorporated bars that are open to the general public (but these must be licensed to offer such a service).

Categories of ownership and management

Free house

A free house is an independently owned pub with no commercial tie to any particular brewery. It is therefore free to choose the beers and other drinks that it stocks.

Tied house

A tied house is a pub that is usually rented from or mortgaged to a brewery, which controls the supply of drinks. At one time this meant that the landlord could only buy beer from that brewery. Although legislation now forces breweries to offer a selection of alternatives (via a guest list), this list is limited and the landlord often pays a high premium for the beer that he could otherwise obtain much more cheaply. The concept of a tie has long been controversial, and for this reason is banned in some countries. In the UK, further recent legislation has sought to open up the market a little more and reduce the powers of the big breweries and "Pubcos" (companies that own a chain of pubs).

Manager

A pub manager is simply an employee of the brewery, contracted to run the pub on the latter's behalf. The manager has a fixed income, usually supplemented by bonuses linked to sales.

Tenant

A tenant rents the pub from the brewery and is bound by a tenancy agreement. This subjects him to the conditions imposed on a tied house, as discussed above.

---

1. Recently seriously damaged by fire.

Appendix II

Index of Pubs Featured

Index of establishments featured in the narrative. Those in bold type indicate that pubs/hotels were still open – and serving alcohol to the public – as at September 2016

The Book of Syn

Russell Thorndike, Dr Syn and the Romney Marsh

By Keith Swallow

The Reverend Christopher Syn, Doctor of Divinity, was a man of many parts: Vicar of Dymchurch; swordsman and duellist; ruthless pirate; smuggler; and murderer. His exploits are so embedded in the culture of Dymchurch and the wider Romney Marsh that many people are unaware that he was a fictional character, the creation of Russell Thorndike.

Thorndike himself lived a life almost as full as that of his chief character; he was a Shakespearian actor, raconteur and bon viveur, as well as a prolific writer and historian. That many believe that Syn once walked the earth is down to Thorndike's ability to weave so much reality into his tales.

However, Syn's existence extends beyond Thorndike's seven novels. There have been three films (including versions by both Disney and Hammer) and Syn has appeared on the stage, in musicals and in comics. There is also a bi-annual 'Day of Syn' held in Dymchurch – the largest free festival in the South of England.

This book explores the life, times and influences of author Russell Thorndike; the Syn novels, films and plays; the realities of smuggling at the time that the novels were set; and the places on Romney Marsh that captivated and inspired Thorndike.

ISBN: 978-0-9548390-9-3
Price: £16 from any good bookshop
(or contact enquiries@eps-edge.demon.co.uk)

Also from
Edgerton Publishing Services

Pett in Sussex, by John Taylor, 2004, ISBN 978-0-9548390-0-0 (0-9548390-0-5) Price £15.00 – A history of the village.

A Changing Shore, An Illustrated Account of Winchelsea Beach, by Michael and Ruth Saville, 2006, ISBN 978-0-9548390-2-4, Price £12.00 – A history of this seaside community, covering also the Mary Stanford lifeboat disaster, Smeaton's Harbour and the Rye Harbour Nature Reserve.

A Survivor's Story, Prisoner of War to Parish Priest, by John Read, 2007, ISBN 978-0-9548390-3-1, Price £10.00 – Prisoner of the Japanese on the infamous Burma Railway and subsequently Rector of Pett, John Read tells his story with a remarkable lack of bitterness.

A Destiny Defined, Dante Gabriel Rossetti and Elizabeth Siddal in Hastings, by Jenny Ridd, 2008, ISBN 978-9548390-4-8, Price £10.00 – The story of the poet/painter and his muse during their happy days in Hastings, where they were married. The book goes on to consider the later, less happy, times.

My Early Years Down Under, by John (Jack) Edge, 2011 (revised edition), ISBN 978-0-9548390-8-6, Price £12.50 – An autobiographical account of an English migrant trying to find work in Western Australia at the beginning of the Great Depression, 1929–1930.

The Jewish Ghost – Being German: A Search for Meaning, by Louise Illig-Mooncie, 2013, ISBN 978-0-9548390-6-2, Price £9.99 – One woman's search for meaning in post-war, post-Holocaust Germany.

Pett à Manger, A Village Cookbook, compiled by Wendy Norcott, 2015 (second edition), ISBN 978-0-9933203-0-9, Price £8.00

The Viking Farm, by Unn Pedersen, 2016. ISBN 978-82-05-49695-8. Price £17.99 – Stories based on archaeology. A girl from the town visits her cousin on the farm.

The Viking Town, by Unn Pedersen, 2016. ISBN 978-82-05-49696-5. Price £17.99 – Stories based on archaeology. A boy from the farm visits his cousin in the town.

Available from any good bookshop
(or contact enquiries@eps-edge.demon.co.uk)